THE NEW
SUBVERSIVES

The New
SUBVERSIVES

Anti-Americanism
of the Religious Right

DANIEL C. MAGUIRE

091726

CONTINUUM / NEW YORK

To Rabbi Francis Barry Silberg
and
Reverend Mary Ann Neevel

1982

The Continuum Publishing Company
575 Lexington Avenue
New York, N.Y. 10022

Printed in the United States of America

Library of Congress Cataloging in Publication Data

Maguire, Daniel C.
The new subversives.

Includes bibliographical references.
1. United States—Politics and government—1977–1981.
2. United States—Politics and government—1981–
3. United States—Moral conditions.   4. Conservatism—
United States—History—20th century.   5. Evangelicalism
—United States—History—20th century.   6. Fundamentalism.   7. Christianity and politics.   I. Title.
E872.M24   320.5′5′0973   82-1576
ISBN 0-8264-0189-9   AACR2

CONTENTS

Acknowledgments

I owe abundant gratitude to the following:

Rabbi Francis Barry Silberg, Senior Rabbi of Congregation Emanu-El B'ne Jeshurun in Milwaukee, who initiated the idea to found Moral Alternatives, an organization to counter the radical right, and invited me to serve as one of its directors;

Reverend Mary Ann Neevel, Minister, Plymouth Church–United Church of Christ, who is co-director of Moral Alternatives and a wise friend;

Justus George Lawler, who urged me to write this book and held me to his unrealistic deadline;

Marjorie Reiley Maguire who thought Lawler's deadline realistic and who read and repaired and suggested and cajoled until the work was done;

Lorna Rixmann who typed the manuscript with stunning accuracy in five days just before Christmas;

Edmond Reiley, my father-in-law, friend, and clipping service;

Anne Mackin, Frances Leap, and Patrick Coy for suggestions, encouragement, and proofreading;

Thomas Worcestor, my Marquette University teaching assistant, who often gave me the gift of time;

Elaine Doyle and Kathleen Butt who supported Moral Alternatives with wisdom and work, and who were remunerated only by their consciences, and

my three brothers and three sisters who have been my teachers since I was a toddler.

Introduction:
BORN AGAIN FASCISTS

The right wing is rising today with an abundance of publicity. Some people belittle the importance of it all, seeing it as a transient aberration, puffed up and sensationalized by the press. It is bobbing to the surface now, they say, but it will soon be absorbed in the mainstream of sanity. Others, while a bit put off by the excesses and pieties of the right, are relieved that some people at least are trying to respond to the collapse of morals in our society. Others see in the New Rightism a powerful, ongoing, and well-financed movement of many intersecting interests that poses a distinct threat to the American way. It is the purpose of this book to show that the latter group is correct, and to suggest what can be done about this phenomenon. These radical rightists, with a flag in one hand and a Bible in the other, have plans for our future, and we ignore them at our peril.

Who are the "New Right?" The term was coined in 1975. They are a motley group of ultraconservative, self-defined "Christian fundamentalists" who decided that the United States was losing its heritage, and so have roared into the political arena to make what they see as the law of God the law of the land. The Moral Majority, founded by Jerry Falwell, is the best-known of the New Right organizations, but there is a great variety of other groups in their entourage. They include the Religious Roundtable, Christian Voice, the Library Court, the National Conservative Political Action

1

Committee, the Committee for the Survival of a Free Congress, the Heritage Foundation, and others. Some of these groups are more concerned with certain issues than others, but they have all found strength in cooperation and are hanging together in a shaky, but still effective, coalition. And they are rich. Falwell and direct-mail expert Richard Viguerie represented this coalition, which raised more money for their candidates in the 1980 elections than did the entire Democratic party nationally. Viguerie has a direct-mail system that reaches four-and-a-half million conservative contributors. The fund raising is computerized and efficient. Parts of the message boom out over thirty religious TV stations, a thousand radio stations, and four religious networks. The top ten TV ministries bring in fifty to ninety million dollars *each* per year.

The New Right also knows the exhilaration of apparent success. They predicted, contrary to the polls, that the 1980 election would not be a cliff-hanger. They were right. They were influential in the defeat of Senators Dick Clark and Thomas McIntyre in 1978. They claim credit for the downfall of Senators McGovern, Church, Culver, Magnuson, Nelson, Bayh, and Javits—all of whom displeased them and were targeted by them for defeat. They helped defeat the Equal Rights Amendment in fifteen states. They managed to disrupt the White House Conference on the Family and to impede congressional efforts at criminal-code reform. They have been influential in forcing the Federal Communications Commission and the Internal Revenue Service to back down on challenges to religious organizations. And they have established themselves as a major influence in the resurgent Republican party. They are busily registering like-minded persons to vote. They are a dominating factor in American politics, and they plan to stay.

They admit that they are radicals and that they want to change the system. They are not open to discussion or to compromise, since they believe that the Bible supports everything they hold dear. They want a bigger military budget and a tougher America. They are building their own schools at a purported rate of several a day and are out to intimidate public schools and libraries that dispense something other than the New Right doctrine. They want to make all abortions illegal and to allow discrimination against homosexual citizens. They hate unions as much as they hate pornography. In the most unsubtle way, they are anti-Semitic, racist, and anti-Catholic. They fear modernity and are out to turn the clock back to what they consider to have been a more godly time.

Their use of language is befuddling. They claim to be conservative, but they want to change the traditional American system of checks and balances. They claim to be evangelical Christians, but most evangelicals reject them. They claim to be fundamentalists, but they miss the crucial fundamentals of the Bible and are fixated on biblical side issues. They claim to be freedom-loving Americans, yet they would censor what others may read in the library and see on television. They claim to be American patriots, but their spirit is fascistic and authoritarian.

Whatever the New Right is, it is now part of American politics. One cannot be interested in politics and ignore the New Rightists. It is possible, however, to make three dangerous errors in assessing this revival of the radical religious-political right: 1) we could overestimate them, ignoring their weaknesses, and fall into paranoia; 2) we could underestimate them and ignore the power they are amassing; 3) we could make scapegoats of them, missing the fact that their writhings are symptomatic of real problems in our society. It is the purpose of this book to avoid these errors. For some initial consolation, let us turn first to the cracks in the New Right.

Chapter One

POLITICS
OF THE ABSURD

T he New Right is not almighty. It seems necessary to say that. Born-again politics arrived on the political scene at a time of terrible dullness. They found the center stage empty and filled it with raucous hoopla and the magic of instant success. *Newsweek* announced: "They are winning."[1] The first chapter of Richard Viguerie's book is entitled "Why the New Right is Winning."[2] The Congress of the United States has reacted with numbness and passivity to the President who endorsed the New Right in his campaign—and who was endorsed by them. It would seem as if the die is cast. We can only watch the dawning of the New Right age.

The first temptation to be guarded against is *paranoia*. Paranoia is an old-time resident of American politics. It affects right, left, and center. It proceeds from an overreaction to what may be a genuine threat. Paranoia endows the threat with demonic powers, and thus makes us less able to counter the real danger. As a noted analyst of political paranoia put it almost twenty years ago, paranoia makes us think of the enemy as possessing "some especially effective source of power: he controls the press; he directs the public mind through 'managed news'; he has unlimited funds; he has a new secret for influencing the mind; he has a special technique for seduction; he is gaining a stranglehold on the educational system."[3] Some reactors to the radical right see all of that in this

5

new phenomenon. Therefore, before examining their actual power—and it is considerable—it is well to look soberly at their debits—and they are also considerable. First of all, the New Right is funny. Laughter redeems, and we shouldn't miss out on it. Secondly, the New Right is loaded with contradictions that need public attention. Finally, the New Right shows some early signs of coming apart at the seams.

Operation Fiasco

On a simple scale of ridiculousness the New Rightists rank high. They combine all the elements of exquisite farce. Sadly for those who value religious experience, much that is funny about them comes from the deviant "Christian" fundamentalism that thoroughly animates the movement. This kind of deviant fundamentalism has always had a flair for a kind of comedy of the absurd. Some thought this had died away after the Scopes trial of 1925. John Scopes, a biology teacher, was put on trial in Dayton, Tennessee for violating state law by teaching the theory of evolution. The trial became a test of fundamentalism in the face of modernity. It was an epic moment of theatric absurdity not easily recaptured. H.L. Mencken's account of that event half a century ago serves to highlight the absurd-comic possibilities of all deviant fundamentalism. He summed up the overall scene as "an obscenity of the very first calibre."[4] His further descriptions fill that bill. "There was a friar wearing a sandwich sign announcing that he was the Bible champion of the world. There was a Seventh Day Adventist arguing that Clarence Darrow was the beast with the seven heads and ten horns described in Revelation XIII, and that the end of the world was at hand. There was an evangelist made up like Andy Gump, with the news that atheists in Cincinnati were preparing to descend upon Dayton, hang the eminent Judge Raulston, and burn the town. There was the ancient who maintained that no Catholic could be a Christian. There was the eloquent Dr. T.T. Martin of Blue Mountain, Mississippi, come to town with a truckload of torches and hymn-books to put Darwin in his place. There was a singing brother bellowing apocalyptic hymns. . . . Dayton was having a roaring time."[5] Then some years later, there was Carl McIntire who got fired up about the evils of communism and led the feisty project to send a million gas-filled balloons, each of them six feet in diameter, across the iron curtain carrying portions of the Bible. In his *Christian Crusade* magazine he blamed the civil rights movement on the communists and argued that the postal zip code system was a Soviet plot.[6]

The spirit of those times is not dead. The House Judiciary Committee heard testimony recently on the subject of prayer in the public schools. Television evangelist James Robison spelled out for Congress the "plagues" that descended upon our nation after the banning of prayer in schools by the Supreme Court in 1962–1963. The Vietnam war accelerated; prominent leaders were assassinated; there followed "escalation of crime, disintegration of families, racial conflict, teen-age pregnancies and venereal disease."[7] All of this from banning prayer in public schools. California evangelist Bill Bright, like Robison, also believed that the Supreme Court's ban on school prayers could be blamed for "crime, racial conflict, drug abuse, political assassinations, the Vietnam war, sexual promiscuity and the demise of American family life."[8] (One wonders what caused calamities when school prayer was still in.)

One might marvel at the liberality of a society that stages such comedy in a hearing room of the House of Representatives, but the humor should not be missed. It was not missed by University of Chicago professor Martin Marty. He wryly noted that after people started wearing yellow "smile buttons," the rate of venereal disease increased. He also pointed out that "the divorce rate rose shortly after the invention of the electronic church . . . when born-again celebrities started writing born-again autobiographies, teenage pregnancies increased; and when fundamentalists started writing sex manuals, the Vietnam war accelerated . . . and executive crime increased right after America decided that God was *not* dead."[9]

All of us, liberal or conservative, bring our absurdities with us when we enter the political arena. Absurdities do not disenfranchise us. But they should not be overlooked. It is the indispensable political function of the jester to find them out and expose them to the appropriate response. Laughter chastens politics and exorcizes society's devils.

There are other examples of the fun the radical religionists bring to us. They are not just gloom boomers bombarding us with their "hit lists" of objectionable politicians and their unctuous, tedious sermonizings. James Wright, executive director of the Maryland Moral Majority, starred in an Annapolis comedy. It seems that a certain bakery was purveying gingerbread men and women with large smiles and prominent sex organs. Sales were brisk, and probably became brisker when Wright sniffed out the cookies. He sent two youngsters in to purchase the gingerbread images, and then charged that the store had sold obscene material to minors. The case failed when the assistant state attorney found the action unsavory but not illegal. It did lead some to wonder whether attempts would soon follow to introduce the "Antipornographic Gingerbread Persons Act" into Maryland law.

The humor of the radical religious right rises to high places. According to a report in *The Wall Street Journal*, Interior Secretary James Watt was being quizzed by the House Interior Committee about whether he really favored preserving wilderness areas for the benefit of "future generations." Watt stunned his questioners by bringing in his millenarian fundamentalist faith as a basis of policy. He avowed, without a blink: "I do not know how many future generations we can count on before the Lord returns."[10] Admittedly, as here, the comic often touches on the tragic. Mr. Watt's private faith that there is little need to fret over future generations, because Jesus will be along to take care of things, may be harmless as a private belief. It is comedy transmuted into tragedy when it provides the basis for cabinet-level policy.

Other such tragicomic voices are heard around us, and should be highlighted. When the Reverend Greg Dixon, National Secretary of the Moral Majority, said that the Moral Majority is a philosophical movement designed to return a right-wing God to government, when Reverend Bailey Smith, President of the Southern Baptist Convention, tells us that God Almighty does not hear the prayers of a Jew, when Dan Fore, former head of the Moral Majority in New York, lets us know that Jews have an almost supernatural power to make money, or that "Christians" can't be blamed for the Inquisition because it was done by "Catholics," when an "inerrant" Bible tells the same folks to get into politics today that it used to tell to stay out, or when they try to write it into law that a newly fertilized ovum is a citizen of the United States, we must laugh as an act of political sanity. And we have to hail the pundits and cartoonists who perform a civil service by bringing this twisted humor to the light of day.

All of this is cited here to stress the point that the right-wing juggernaut is missing some of its essential parts. It is too deep in ridiculousness to be almighty.

Contradictions of the Righteous Right

In a democracy, all must be welcomed into the political process, but the intellectual baggage one brings to that process is open to inspection by everyone else. All have a right to know just how much mental disarray one is bringing into the world of power and politics. Political debate deserves intellectual rigor, since it is in this arena that decisions are made about who will eat and who will go hungry, about who will live and who will die. One's credentials must be up front and on call when entering politics to influence what goes on there.

There is much that is weak in the internal "logic" of the movement. Its discourse is riddled with conflicting positions. It speaks from one side of the mouth and then from the other. In short, it is not coherent.

Pseudoconservatism

Given the simplistic either/or mentality of the New Rightists, one is either "liberal" or "conservative." They are manifestly not "liberal." Therefore they conclude that they are "conservative." That is a key assumption of the New Right, and one of their biggest lies.

Even their rhetoric shows that their claim to conservative status is shaky. They talk of "taking control" of the conservative movement, implying that there is a conservatism other than theirs that needs controlling. They also bicker with other conservatives, and express fears that even the conservative President Reagan, who delights them in most things, may stray from their conservative orthodoxy. At times, they even come right out and blatantly show their counterconservative hand. New Right leader Paul Weyrich says: "We are radicals who want to change the existing power structure . . . the New Right does not want to conserve, we want to change—we *are* the forces of change."[11]

The pseudoconservative phenomenon is not new. Pseudoconservatives have been described as persons who, "although they believe themselves to be conservatives and usually employ the rhetoric of conservatism, show signs of a serious and restless dissatisfaction with American life, traditions and institutions. They have little in common with the temperate and compromising spirit of true conservatism in the classical sense of the word. . . . Their political reactions express rather a profound if largely unconscious hatred of our society and its ways. . . ."[12] As another study put it: "The pseudo-conservative is a man who, in the name of upholding traditional American values and institutions and defending them against more or less fictitious dangers, consciously or unconsciously aims at their abolition."[13]

From this distrust of our traditions and structures flows the "amend the Constitution" syndrome, so obvious in pseudoconservative moments of American history. In the early fifties, when a pseudoconservative mood was in high fever, one hundred amendments to the Constitution were introduced in the eighty-third

Congress. It is interesting to note what these proposed amendments were up to: to limit nonmilitary expenditures, to repeal the
income tax, to bar all federal expenditures for "the general welfare," to redefine treason, etc. As one observer put it: "The sum
total of these amendments could easily serve to send the whole
structure of American society crashing to the ground."[14]

In our day, Congress has before it some thirty similarly subversive bills to limit sharply the power of the federal judiciary. These
bills spring from the New Right's discontent with the decisions the
Supreme Court has made over the last two decades in areas such
as mandatory prayer in public schools, a woman's right to abortion,
and busing to end segregated education. The radically subversive
thrust of these amendments is signaled by U.S. Court of Appeals
Judge Irving R. Kaufman. These bills, he says, threaten "not only
a number of individual liberties, but also the very independence
of the Federal courts, an independence that has safeguarded the
rights of American citizens for nearly 200 years."[15] Such radical
tinkering with the system is not conservative. It represents an attempted subversion of the method of checks and balances that was
so central to the vision of the founding fathers and to that of true
conservatives. These radical rightists are not conservative. That is
their first and most basic contradictory claim.

Religious Tests in Politics

There are a number of other contradictions in the New Right.
They proclaim the doctrine of the separation of church and state,
and yet they impose religious, "Bible-based" tests on political candidates. These religious tests or checklists show little concern for
the major political issues of peace and social justice. They are,
rather, little catechisms of deviant fundamentalist faith. It is their
goal to elect candidates who measure up to their religious criteria
and thus, by majority vote, make their fundamentalist faith the law
of the land. This goes contrary to the core purpose of the nonestablishment of religion—which later came to be called the separa-

tion of church and state. The radical rightists accept the rhetoric of separation, but are fully occupied in frustrating its purposes.

A twofold advantage was seen by the founding fathers of the United States in the nonestablishment of religion: government could not intrude on the privacy and integrity of religious bodies, and no religious persuasion could be imposed by law on citizens who enjoyed other beliefs.

It was the American ideal not to put government behind any sectarian religious views. Thomas Jefferson prized religious freedom. But he clearly differed from today's moral majoritarians on how freedom and religion should relate in the American plan. True religion, he said, should not be propagated by "temporal punishments" and "civil incapacitations," but "by its influence on reason alone." He warned against those governments where rulers and legislators "being themselves but fallible and uninspired men, have assumed dominion over the faith of others, setting up their own opinions and modes of thinking as the only true and infallible, and as such endeavoring to impose them on others. . . ."[16] Where persons can impose their private religious interpretations on others by force of law, said Jefferson, the result is "hypocrisy and meanness."[17] Once again, Jefferson, sounding like he saw the Moral Majority and others emerging, wrote: "Our civil rights have no dependence on our religious opinions, any more than our opinions in physics or geometry; and therefore the proscribing of any citizen as unworthy of the public confidence by laying upon him an incapacity of being called to offices of trust or emolument, unless he profess or renounce this or that religious opinion, is depriving him injudiciously of those privileges and advantages to which, in common with his fellow-citizens, he has a natural right. . . . It tends also to corrupt the principles of that very religion it is meant to encourage, by bribing with monopoly of worldly honours and emoluments, those who will externally profess and conform to it. . . ." Jefferson adds that "though indeed these are criminals who do not withstand such temptation, yet neither are those innocent who lay the bait in their way."[18]

This was the foundational dream of the United States. No particular religious views will be "established." Religions will make their appeals in freedom to the reasoned judgment of free persons. Ideals and principles bred of religious experience are free to compete for political expression, but no one bias shall work its way into law in such a way that legitimately debated differences are suppressed. Even the religious views of the majority will not become official. Majority rule with minority rights is the American ideal.

Ideals, of course, are not sweetly and easily realized. For a long period evangelical Protestantism did enjoy unofficial establishment status. Still, the ideal is clear and it is the soul of the separation doctrine.

The New Rightists oppose this American ideal. For all their talk about separation, they want establishment status for their religious views. Jerry Falwell, the founder of the Moral Majority, is not ambiguous on this point. This nation "was founded by godly men upon godly principles *to be a Christian nation.*" [19] The unecumenical nature of his sentiments is not in doubt. "If a person is not a Christian, he is inherently a failure. . . ." [20] By "Christian" Pastor Falwell means his kind of "Christian." It does not include civil rights advocates, peace activists, environmentalists, feminists, supporters of civil rights for homosexuals or abortions for poor women, etc. It is Falwell's subcultural, right-wing Christianity that would be the mark of his "Christian" America. Religion's gentle appeal to reason, as championed by Jefferson, would be replaced by coercion, with "civil incapacitations" visited upon dissenters. The Falwellian hunger for majority status is a desire for tyranny of the majority through law. Hence the hit lists and the religious tests of political orthodoxy. The tactic is simple. If you can elect politicians on the basis of a bigoted religious test, you will get a bigoted religious government. Your bias will become unofficially, but effectively, established. The wall of separation will be ruptured. This is the second elementary self-contradiction and weakness in the program of the new religious-political right.

Civil Liberties and Government Intrusion

There are other contradictions in the position of the rightists. Their rhetoric drips with love of freedom and fear of government encroachment on that freedom. Stripped of its puff and fluff, their prescription is this: freedom (read anarchy) for the elite, and tyranny for women, the poor, libraries and educational institutions, and homosexual citizens.

The most extreme libertarian views are held by the New Right as far as business is concerned. Laissez faire freedom is a matter of biblical faith for them. They preach the divine right of free enterprise. With an appalling misunderstanding of biblical literature, Falwell proclaims: "The free enterprise system is clearly outlined in the Book of Proverbs in the Bible. Jesus Christ made it clear that the work ethic was a part of his plan for man."[21] Nothing should impede the free march of business. All inhibiting regulations about worker safety, environmental protection, monopoly busting, affirmative action and, above all, labor unions, must be restrained or abolished in the name of the "conservative" God.

When we move from boardroom to womb, the contradiction emerges without subtlety. Government must be placed on the backs of the pregnant woman. Here there is no laissez faire or individual freedom. A woman who believes that for somber but moral reasons she must terminate a pregnancy must be prohibited by government from exercising her judgment—and this even though a number of religious and ethical authorities support her judgment. Homosexual citizens are to be blocked by law from pursuing certain careers or from seeking legal redress for discrimination. This would allow government to intrude into career choice and self-defense—areas of the most personal and sacred freedom. Libraries must not be free to supply books that offend the narrow canons of deviant fundamentalist faith. Censorship is the first passion of the fascist mind, and it is in full bloom in the New Right. The denial of government funds is the preferred weapon of the New Right to bludgeon institutions of learning and health care that do not hew to the right-wing checklist of virtues.

A student of civil liberty in the United States described the ideals of our country this way: *"The essence of civil liberty is the right to be wrong.* That is, the civil right to be wrong, not necessarily the moral right, or the intellectual right. Civil liberties deny *to the government* the authority to determine what is right or true in theology, economics, biology, diet, or political theory. Unless you believe in your opponent's *civil right* to be wrong, you cannot really believe in your *civil right* to be right, but only in your *power* to be right."[22]

The New Right dissents from this ideal. For them, error has no rights. And "error" is disagreement with them on the things they take seriously. Business, of course, which God wishes to be untrammeled in its freedom, is free to be wrong. It is not to be inhibited if it strays. Educators, librarians, women, gay persons, and political officers who disagree with the radical right do not have a right to be wrong. For such as these, the New Right, not freedom, shall reign.

Pro-Israel/Anti-Semitic

Illogic arises again in the attitude of the New Right toward Jews. In what is a tour de force of absurdity, the New Right manages to be at once pro-Israel and anti-Semitic. The New Rightists come on like Israel's best friends. But friends like this Israel, and Jews everywhere, do not need. Israel is important to the religious rightists, but not for its own sake. Using the Bible as they do, as a kind of ouija board to predict the future, Israel is in a starring role. Through a fanciful reading of the Hebrew prophets, New Right seers like Hal Lindsey, in his best seller *The Late Great Planet Earth*, show the place of Israel in the rightist scheme of things. Lindsey gives us the most detailed version of the millenarian faith, which, in various forms, suffuses the religious soul of the right.

In the gospel according to Lindsey, the prophets saw the future and spelled it out with incredible exactitude. As we near the end of history, in this view, certain configurations of national power will appear as signals of the impending end and the coming of

Jesus. The Common Market will be formed as a new Rome. Russia will rise militarily. The United States will become a Christian nation and the light of the world. But at center stage is Israel. "All of this would be around the most important sign of all—that is the Jew returning to the land of Israel after thousands of years of being dispersed. The Jew is the most important sign to this generation."[23]

That is why large segments of the evangelical Christian world have been in such a tizzy since the establishment of Israel as a nation. They believe that the excitement of the "latter days" is upon us. The millennium is at hand.

Judaism, Israel, and Jews in general are of major importance—but only as signals of the Christian triumph that is to be. Israel is valued only as the staging ground for the return of Jesus, at which point, of course, the only good Jew will be a Christianized Jew. There is simply no respect in the radical right for the authenticity of Jewish religious experience. The Jews are either pawns in the revelation of millennial bliss expected for Christians, or they are grist for the mills of conversion. Jews as Jews are literally damnable. God would not even hear their prayers, as the Reverend Bailey Smith pointed out to us in a moment of candor concerning the right's assessment of Jews. Only prayers offered in the name of Jesus get through to God.

Falwell at first agreed with Smith on this, but then, after a hurried conference with Rabbi Marc Tannenbaum, Falwell (and apparently God) had a change of mind. In a politic statement, Falwell restored Jewish access to God in prayer.[24] Falwell's conversion here, however, could only be verbal. In the hard-nosed fundamentals of his creed, neither a Jew nor anyone else can bypass Jesus en route to God. Jews, after all, are not "born again," and in Falwellian theology, that leaves them religiously dead.

Prolife/Prodeath

The contradictions do not end. It is no simple matter to catalogue them all. The New Right is on the one hand prolife, and on the other hand, prodeath. They are prolife in a very limited sense and are prodeath in a potentially unlimited sense. "Prolife" is sloganese for being unqualifiedly antiabortion. The rightists do not just favor fetuses, however. They also sacralize life after birth—for upwardly mobile white people.

Black life is of concern to the "prolife" forces of the New Right only in its prenatal state, since that would come under the abortion ban that the New Right wants to put into law. After birth, the life of blacks seems to be of little importance. The self-designated "prolifers" of the New Right take no note of the fact that in the United States at this time a black woman is three times more likely than a white woman to die in childbirth and twice as likely to lose her infant in the first year of its life. If the black child survives, he or she is five times more likely to be murdered than a white child. None of this impresses the new "Christian" right. In their brand of mean-spirited individualism, "them that gets deserves." Thus, blacks, who are not getting, are getting what they deserve. If blacks would seek help for their lives, they will have to look outside the "prolife" lobby of the New Right. The poor in general should be similarly advised. Their plight is something to which members of the New Right seem blind. Phyllis Schlafly, for example, while championing family life and the need for women to stay at home, is apparently unaware that there are women too poor not to have to work.

The prodeath bias of the New Right shows up even more in their attitude toward "defense" than it does in their disdain of blacks and the poor. The New Right is more militant than the Joint Chiefs of Staff. They weep over America's military impotence. They are scarcely satisfied now with President Reagan's proposal to spend 1.5 trillion dollars over the next five years for weapons—which comes to 34 million dollars per hour. They are unimpressed with the fact that if you gave the annual defense budget for the year 1979 to Jesus Christ, he could have spent one hundred thousand dollars a day from the day he was born right up to today, and still have 750 years of spending left. These massive expenditures for war do not slake their military thirsts. The logic of their position seems to be that only an invulnerable first-strike capability would keep us safe.

As I shall explain further in chapter four, the rightists need a war, just as they needed the foundation of Israel. Nuclear war squares nicely with some of the scriptural language about the fiery tribulation that will inaugurate the "latter days"—the big chastening blast that will set the stage for Jesus's triumphant return. There is a dangerous *need* for nuclear war implicit in the deviant fundamentalism of the New Right. Just as the coming millennium dispenses Interior Secretary Watt from care for future generations, that same millennial hope induces a pious nonchalance in New Right believers. The coming inaugural war will do them no harm. True believers can view this impending judgment with a "not-to-worry" calm. Their faith is their thermonuclear insurance. They will be saved by a blessed "rapture," lifted up to meet Christ "in the air," while the good earth and the unbelievers are scorched in the final holocaust. Those of us who do not carry "rapture" insurance do well to signal the danger when folks like this move into power. Prolife is what the "prolifers" of the New Right are not.

Family vs. Patriarchy

The rightists are also champions of private morality and family life, and yet their heroes are often tarnished by the very standards of the right. The rightists oppose divorce and support permanent marriage. And yet in the 1980 elections the undivorced Jimmy Carter was cast as the villain, and the divorced Ronald Reagan as the saint. Richard Viguerie could even confide to Mr. Reagan: "Your personal example, along with Mrs. Reagan's, can help lead America to a rebirth of greatness."[25] Given their chaste horror of divorce, one might legitimately query: "Which Mrs. Reagan?" Similar delicious ironies are found in the fact that the New Right ratings systems for rigorous churchmen like Representative Paul Simon and Father Robert Drinan gives them a 0 percent, while a Richard

Kelly, of Abscam fame, got a 100 percent rating. Again one senses that their act is not quite together.

The New Right also postures as the last bastion of profamily idealism. They are not. As I shall spell out in chapter five, the Family Protection Act, around which the New Right rallies, is a blueprint for fascist family life. The act is more a Patriarchy Protection Act. Women and children are shortchanged. The family is the place where men rule.

Falwell is quite candid about that. Men are the natural rulers. "Men are the key to a moral revolution in America," says Falwell. "Men have led women and children a long way; now it is time for an 'army' of spiritually concerned men to lead America in the right way." [26] In the Falwellian home, "the father is responsible to exercise spiritual control and to be the head over his wife and children: '. . . Women are to be feminine and manifest the ornament of a meek and quiet spirit, which is in the sight of God a great prize' (Peter 3:4). In the Christian home, the woman is to be submissive; 'wives, submit yourselves unto your own husbands, as unto the Lord' (Ephesians 5:22)." [27] Patriarchy could scarcely be made of sterner stuff, with women submitting to their husbands *as if the husband were God*—"as unto the Lord."

Children are to be no less submissive. They must be taught that the father is boss in the home, and they must follow their mothers' good example and obey. There is recognition that children might resist this, and so the Family Protection Act tightens up the concept of child abuse so that it permits corporal punishment, applied by a parent or an individual authorized by a parent. The Act also senses that wives might not be as submissive as God, Falwell, Senator Laxalt, and the other men of the New Right want, and so it would prohibit the federal government from giving funds or instituting programs to prevent and treat child and spouse abuse, beyond what the states are doing. Runaway shelters are not to offer contraceptive or abortion procedures, or even counseling, without prior parental approval. Parental authority in this view is paternal authority, and is decidedly muscular in tone. No wife or child could see this as "profamily." Again, the rhetoric and the reality are at odds.

Religious Contradictions

Religiously, too, the New Right is shot through with contradictions. On the one hand, they express an unqualified trust in God: "If God is on our side," Falwell incants, "no matter how militarily superior the Soviet Union is, they could never touch us. God would miraculously protect America."[28] That pious confidence hardly squares with the martial lusts they manifest for more and more missiles and nuclear kill-power.

They claim to be pro-Pope and pro-Catholic, but they never quote the popes on issues of peace or justice, and often their rhetoric slips and they reveal themselves as the children of the anti-Romanist Protestants of the last century. They claim that theirs is the very essence of evangelical faith, yet most evangelicals disavow them. Even many self-styled "fundamentalists" view them with disapproval. They proclaim the Bible to be inerrant and accessible to anyone of good will, but they disagree on its meaning with most biblical students, Christian and Jewish.

In short, the New Rightists are eccentric and self-contradictory. Here are people who would die for the Panama Canal but would not stir for civil rights, who seem to fear orgasms more than slaughters, who wrap themselves with flag and Bible and contradict both. Paranoia in the face of them can be cured by a closer look.

The Fragile Coalition

One way to avoid paranoia is to experience the paranoia of your adversaries and to see what it is doing to them. The New Right is not likely to enjoy enduring unity for the simple reason that no one can unite a group of paranoids. The New Right is not a political party—though it is having considerable success in coopting the Republican party. Much less is it a coherent intellectual movement. On the contrary, it is a loose melange of uncoordinated interests clustered around shared fears and hates, with no intellectually framed common ground. As a classically paranoid movement, it contains within itself the seeds of its own disintegration.

The deviant evangelicalism that infuses the New Right comes from a tradition of fear. For them history is an unfolding conspiracy. One or more species of conspiring evil is always after them. Over time it has been such divergent demons as Masons, Romanists, Jesuits, Jews, the international bankers' syndicate, Eddyites, secular humanists, or communists. Basically the enemy is modernism. The trusted simplicities of the past are under assault by it and the fundamentalist wagons have formed a circle to ward it off. The chaos and frenzy suggested by that metaphor are inherent in the New Right. It is a situation in which something has to give, in which precarious unity yields easily to fragmentation.

The Religious Split

The New Right is religious. Even the activist fund raiser Richard Viguerie ends his book *The New Right: We're Ready to Lead* with a call for a national day of prayer and fasting. It's the "Christian America" crowd back at it. This means that though they do not have an intellectual platform—they have little time for political theory or for the more reasoned expressions of Christian religion—they do have a Bible. It is their foundation and their base. And it can also prove their undoing. The interpretation of the Bible by the radical religious right is eccentric and bizarre, and it separates them from a majority of other people of the book. Falwell begins his book *Listen America!* with the statistic that there are sixty million "born-again" Christians. This figure is deceptive, as are the larger figures sometimes used by the religious right to claim majority status. The evangelical community is very diverse. A Gallup poll published in *Newsweek* in September 1980 showed this division: left of center, 20 percent; at the center, 31 percent; right of center, 37 percent. At that time, 52 percent of evangelicals were for Carter and 31 percent for Reagan. That figure changed before

November, but the picture is not one of a solid front of right-wing evangelical Christians such as Falwell implies. Moreover, 53 percent in this poll supported the highly symbolic ERA.

Evangelicals are those who rest their faith on the Bible, who believe in a transforming experience of the Holy Spirit, and who are committed to missionary work—"evangelism." These generic characteristics obviously admit of a variety of species. Falwellian fundamentalists cannot claim to be the voice of all evangelicals. Rather, as Cullen Murphy said, "fundamentalism is merely a subculture within 'mainstream' evangelicalism, a relatively young and extreme movement within an older, moderate one." [29]

The term "fundamentalist" was coined in 1920. As George Marsden, a student of the fundamentalist phenomenon, puts it: "Fundamentalists were evangelical Christians, close to the traditions of the dominant American revivalist establishment of the nineteenth century, who in the twentieth century militantly opposed both modernism in theology and the cultural changes that modernism endorsed." [30] This "modernism" was seen as undermining the biblical foundations of the United States and importing "atheistic" ideas such as Darwinism. In reaction, the fundamentalists insisted on the divine inspiration of every word of the Bible, and added to this a confidence in the imminent second coming of Jesus. Fundamentalism never was homogeneous, and surely is not so today. Many who call themselves fundamentalists distance themselves from Falwellian fundamentalism. Falwell and Company, then, did not start out with a seamless robe of born-again right wingers. Evangelical Christianity is a rich and variegated phenomenon.

Not all evangelicals believe in the inerrancy of the Bible in all matters, nor are all evangelicals so fearfully reactive against modern culture and critical religious scholarship. Hence many of them are rising in indignation at the caricature of Christianity professed by the new religious right. Jim Wallis, editor of *Sojourners*, a liberal evangelical journal, points out that the gospel that Jesus preached was good news for the poor, but that the gospel of the New Right fundamentalists is no such thing. "Evangelicals in our day are not known as friends of the poor. Rather, evangelicals are known to have a decided preference for the successful and prosperous who see their wealth as a sign of God's favor. Ironically, a movement which once fought to free slaves, support industrial workers and liberate women, now has a reputation for accommodating to racism, favoring business over labor, and resisting equal rights for women. In our nation's ghettos, barrios and unions, evangelicals are generally not regarded as allies."[31]

If anything, the stridency and bias of the New Right religionists is tilting other evangelicals in the opposite direction. Billy Graham, in an article entitled "A Change of Heart," admits that he had too much identified the Kingdom of God with the American way of life—the precise error of Falwellian Christians. He criticizes the use for massive armaments of resources that could otherwise be used to alleviate human suffering and hunger. He supports the SALT disarmament efforts, and does not think that present differences with the Soviets are worth a nuclear war.[32] All that puts him at a considerable distance from Falwellian Christians, and even from the earlier Billy Graham. Other Christians are criticizing the Friedmanian economics of the new religious rightists. (Milton Friedman is quoted by Falwell almost as often as the Bible.) John Coleman Bennett, former president of Union Theological Seminary in New York, writes: "The economic doctrine of the Moral Majority is in absolute contradiction to the economic teachings of ecumenical Protestantism in most of this century and to the economic teaching of Roman Catholicism in many centuries. This is especially true of Catholic teachings concerning limits on the use of private property."[33]

Aside from the religious differences of the New Right with much of Christianity, the neoconservative intellectuals who marched with them toward the Reagan victory are now embarrassed by their company and want out. These neoconservatives, who write for *Commentary* and frequent the Georgetown Center for International and Strategic Studies, have little relish for the company of people who think the earth was created in six twenty-four hour days, and who find all major modern events predicted in the ancient pages of the Bible. The antiintellectualism of the New Right is offensive to neoconservative highbrows, who are now anxious to belittle the influence of the religious zealots. This can only offend the "we're ready to lead" mindset of the Vigueries, Falwells, and LaHayes. Here too, the coalition is uneasy.

Issues that Divide

New Right unity is imperiled on another front also. The *issues* they have centered on have the potential to split even the true believers. Martin Marty argues wisely that "American pluralism has too many counterforces to yield to this new fundamentalist right wing all that it wants."[34] If a school prayer amendment passed, the fray would begin about what the prayer would be. Some favor quiet meditation, some a reading of scripture, or prayers offered in the name of Jesus—which, remember, for the fundamentalists are the only prayers that are heard by God. And what about areas where Mormons or Jews predominate? If the prayer is so innocuous as not to offend Jews, Mormons, or Christians of any stripe, would it please anyone? Would it be prayer?

Similarly, there is already division within the movement on the tactics appropriate to banning abortion. Should there be a Human Life Amendment? Which of the many versions offered should it be? There is division on how many exceptions should be allowed, if any. Some antiabortionists prefer a "States Rights" Amendment, which would allow the states to ban abortion. Of course, it is already recognized that not all states would do so. And so antiabortionists dispute among themselves. It was Dante who said: "When two men are fighting, the third party may watch with contentment." Those who would like to see abortion law reflect the breadth of ethical debate on the subject will have increasingly more to watch with contentment as the abortion prohibitionists battle and divide.

Also, in the November 1980 elections, the New Right lured labor union members to their side with issues such as gun control. Now union members are finding that they may have their guns, but they are losing their jobs, or even their unions. The virulent antiunion feelings of the New Right will come more to the fore with their very success with unions. The first union to endorse Reagan, PATCO, was the first union to go during the Reagan Administration. That was a loud signal to labor, and if rightist influence prevails, more signals will be forthcoming. Right-wing successes here may lead to new and important coalitions. Suddenly union workers, who in the 1960s found little in common with campus life, may find common cause with teachers, librarians, and women's groups, and may see the wisdom of a renewed identification with blacks.

There are other issue-related forces for disintegration. Regular Republicans of a more conservative bent may shy more from the New Rightists as their true colors are exposed to light. Also, the New Right's dogmatic interest in Israel will not rest well with conservative businessmen, who on nondogmatic grounds are drawn to the interests of the rich Arab world. The antipornography passion of the New Right may work against them. How many people would really want the Moral Majority to be the supreme court of what constitutes pornography?

Success as Failure

There are other causes of division that exist in the New Right. Billy Graham warned the new evangelists that the most difficult thing in life to handle is "success."[35] Professor David Harrell sums up the temptation this way: "You preach on sin, you warn of the troubles ahead, you pray for the Lord to come, and, my Lord, how the money rolls in."[36] It is a fact of human history, to which not even religion lends immunity, that when money rolls in competition and division follow. Such competition is already in evidence. There is another corollary to big money: commercialism and corruption. One visitor to the Convocation 1981 of New Right evangelists called the event a "sorry circus of crass commercialism."[37] And there is no slight significance in the report of an exultant Tammy Bakker proclaiming on the set in the luxuriously equipped

television studio of PTL (Praise The Lord): "This life is so great—
I just love it whether or not it's true."[38] Religious people can be
slowed in their reach for the pocket when the scent of corruption
arises.

Maybe the reaction against the power of the New Right has already begun. Approval came easily for Supreme Court Justice San-
dra O'Connor from a Senate the New Right had claimed as its
own, in spite of her non-Falwellian record on abortion. Tiffin, Iowa
may have sent another signal of reaction in September 1981, when
voters in the Clear Creek School District turned out in record
numbers—four times that of the preceding year—and soundly rejected a proposal to make the Bible a supplementary textbook. The
spirit of Tiffin may be moving.

Finally, the naive theological pieties of the radical right are out
of season in these United States. Theologian Robert McAfee Brown
refers to their "breathtaking theological arrogance."[39] Even people
of simple piety are put off by these men who run around talking
about God as though they just had lunch with him. Most stomachs
bear poorly with even a little self-righteous pomp. When Jerry
Falwell tells us that God is personally opposed to the ERA, the
question follows naturally: "How do you know that, Jerry?" Even
nonfeminists might moderate their views in self-defensive reaction
against the pontifical fulminatings from the right. Perhaps the causes
most attacked by the New Right may soon begin to say: "With
enemies like this, who needs friends?"

To sum up, the New Right is marked by the classical deformities
of a fanatical movement. It is also at odds with many of the basic
assumptions upon which this nation was founded. But the same
history that condemns the New Rightists also leaves us with a
warning. Weird, loosely connected movements can powerfully alter the course of human events. We do well to assess their power
carefully, and to that I now turn.

Chapter Two

PROSPECTS FOR TRAGEDY

Almost thirty years ago, an astute observer of the American scene wrote that "in a populistic culture like ours . . . in which it is possible to exploit the wildest currents of public sentiment for private purposes, it is at least conceivable that a highly organized, vocal, active and well-financed minority could create a political climate in which the rational pursuit of our well-being and safety would become impossible."[1] He warned further against the simplisms of the radical right, with their perennial fears that total, apocalyptic destruction was at hand. "Unfortunately," he said, "in our time the views of the extreme right have greater capacity for becoming a self-fulfilling prophecy."[2]

This could sound more than a little paranoid until one realizes that these are the words of Richard Hofstadter, the outstanding critic of paranoia in American political life. His predictions were not made lightly. He died in 1970, but people are turning more and more to his writings on the dangers from what he called the "pseudoconservative" right.

For the sake of sanity, and as an exercise in anticipatory revisionism, it is well to be aware of the weaknesses of the New Right that we have seen in the previous chapter. Still, it would not be sane to ignore their strengths. Even short-term strength can do irreversible harm, and the New Right has long-term possibilities.

27

The New Right, for all its foibles and follies, is not negligible. It has definite and formidable strengths.

Obviously the New Right has money and organization, and controls a huge communications network. There is power in all of that. But we won't know their power just by counting their TV stations, radio shows, and dollars. These are only the products of the real motive forces tapped by the New Right. The allure of the right runs deep, and this calls us to some basic reflections on the human psyche and its needs. At this level of analysis, the power of the New Right derives from four principal sources: 1) the need for authority and simplicity in a complicated world; 2) the beckoning power of religious and tribal (patriotic) symbols; 3) the drawing power of fear and hatred; 4) the discovery of real problems that the rest of society is ignoring or belittling.

The Lure of the Oracle

To a world beset with bewildering complexity and startling change, the radical right purveys authority and simplicity. There is no grayness on the right—only darkness or light. There is absolute truth and absolute error, absolute right and absolute wrong. In this perspective, the pain of ambiguity is banished. This meets some fundamental needs, which are no less compelling for their irrationality.

Permit me to illustrate this need with a story. When my son Tommy was two-and-a-half years of age, I came upon him one September afternoon in the den. He was showing his cloth dog "Patches" something outside the window. It suddenly occurred to me that Tommy would not remember the phenomenon of autumn. The previous year he had been otherwise engaged, and had missed the miracle of fall. I pointed to the leaves on the trees outside and asked him their color. "Green!" Then I broke the news, telling him that in a few weeks those leaves would change from being green and would become red, yellow, orange, and brown, and that shortly thereafter they would all fall off the tree and wait there for us to rake them up. Tommy stood there, with Patches in his arms, sucking his thumb, and I wondered if he believed the remarkable prediction I had just made.

The next day I walked past the den, and there was Tommy, repeating my lecture on autumn to Patches. "All leaves green," he announced to his friend. "All leaves turn red, yellow, orange, and brown. Fall down!" Tommy believed me! I realized that in Tommy's almost three-year-old mind, there were two sources of certitude. One was his own sense knowledge. By this, with immediate evidence, he knew that the leaves at that moment were green and that the sky was blue. But Tommy had another source of certitude, no less reliable than immediate sense knowledge—my authority. He was as sure that the leaves would turn to other colors as he was that they were at that moment green. At that level of psychological development, authority and sense knowledge were of equal might and infallibility.

We are born into a quest for meaning and sense. From the moment we are displaced from the comforts of the womb and pushed into a world of chill and noise, of light and shocks, we have to try to make some sense of it. Trust develops during the early months, and as soon as verbal communication ensues, that trust is placed without qualification in our significant sources of authority. Questions pour out toward the oracle-parents. Reliance on authority is our earliest sense-making resource. Even sense experience is secondary to it, because sense experience produces more questions than answers, constantly surprising us with enigmatic and unconnected data. And so we ask, and *we believe.* And until doubts arise regarding our oracles, we enjoy a paradise of oracular certitude. When the oracles betray us—or inconvenience us—we turn to other oracles, or to private interpretation. Eventually, it is hoped, we arrive at critical intelligence, ready to question the oracular presumptions and the regnant orthodoxies of the culture—orthodoxies that are only collective efforts to expand the sense-making task into which we are all commissioned by birth.

However—and here is the rub—there is a pain in maturity and

critical consciousness. In the land of maturity, ambiguity is a tenured resident. We must live with it; it will not be expelled. And yet at some level of our minds we remember the peace of a world where oracles banished all the demons of uncertainty, where predictions that trees would change color always came true, where frightening dreams were explained consolingly—and we hanker to get back there. At some uneasy level of our minds we want to return to those early simplicities.

And so the quest for an oracle is an eternal temptation. Some will find their infallible daddy or mommy in a cult leader, in an "inerrant" Bible, in an "infallible" pope, or in a combination of all of these, such as is found in the new religious-political right. These needs are deep, and whoever seems to meet them has power. We do well not to underestimate that power.

A year after the 1925 Scopes trial and the disgrace of narrow fundamentalism, the distinguished journal *The Christian Century* tolled the knell of the fundamentalist phenomenon. They wondered that "so decisive a rout of fundamentalism was unexpected. . . . Looking at it as an event now passed, anybody should be able to see that the whole fundamentalist movement was hollow and artificial . . . fundamantalism has been a *sport,* an accidental phenomenon making its sudden appearance in our ecclesiastical order, but wholly lacking the qualities of constructive achievement or survival. . . . It is henceforth to be a disappearing quality in American religious life, while our churches go on to larger issues. . . ."[3]

Clearly that demise was prematurely reported. The churches that were to go "on to larger issues" are now in a state of decline. From 1970 to 1980 the United Methodist Church declined by 11.4 percent, the United Presbyterian Church by 22 percent, the Episcopal Church by 16.9 percent and the Christian churches by 22.6 percent.[4] Fundamentalism is blooming, in churches and on television and radio. It is meeting the needs for sure authority and simplicity, and it will again survive those who predict its demise. Oracles we will always have with us, the fundamentalist oracle included. This human desire for an oracle is the first cause of the New Right, "fundamentalist" power.

Tribal Religion

"Everything," said the ancient Thales, "is full of gods." The human animal, even the secularized, sophisticated human animal, will not be without his or her gods. The quest for sacredness, however identified, is built into the species. "Religion" is the term for the quest for the sacred and, whatever form it takes, it has an inner core of fantastic power. In his study of religions Huston Smith says: ". . . whenever religion comes to life it displays a startling quality; it takes over. All else, while not silenced, becomes subdued and thrown without contest into a supporting role."[5] We do well to look with care upon that which comes to us in religious dress. This is especially so if that religion mixes the potent symbolism of the sacred with the passion of tribal patriotism, known today as nationalism. This sets us up for a double-barrelled blast. The New Right uses both barrels.

The history of religions illumines some of the character and strength of the current religious eruption on the right. Arnold Toynbee points up the links between the emotions of the religio-sacred and the fervor of the "super-patriot": "Human beings are inclined to worship the greatest powers that are within their ken. . . ."[6] So it was that early food-gathering people worshipped those things on which they were so utterly dependent. Their gods were earth, water, sun, moon, and those animals or forces of nature that threatened human life. When the wandering of the hunter and gatherer yielded to the collectivization of early civilization, religious as well as economic changes occurred. Human beings became enormously impressed with their collective power. Working in the organized concert of civilization, people could convert jungle swamps into fertile land by building canals and dikes and accomplish other marvelous victories over the power of nature. A new outlook was born when, in Toynbee's words, "the unprecedented productivity of these reclaimed wildernesses had raised the wealth and populousness of a local community from the level of a Neolithic village to the level of a Sumerian city-state."[7]

Toynbee gives impressive evidence that, at the dawn of civilization in Sumer, the nature-gods became political gods. Impressed with the feats of their city-states, the people of that time transferred divinity from nature to the state. Enlil, the wind god, becomes the deification of the state of Nippur. Nanna, the moon god, becomes the personification of the divine state of Ur. Athena, the olive goddess, becomes the deification of Athens, as did the water-god, Poseidon, for Corinth. The volcano god or thunder god, Yahweh, became the deification of the Hebrew people. Toynbee's comment on this is: "The local communities have become divinities, and these divinities that stand for collective human power have become paramount over the divinities that stand for natural forces. The injection of this amount of religious devotion into nationalism has turned nationalism into a religion, and this a fanatical one."[8]

Since nothing is intelligible outside its history, modern nationalism and patriotism can only be understood against the background of the primitive divinization of the state. This divinization took on other colorations. In Toynbee's view, modern nationalism imbibed deeply from the messianic spirit of Christianity, which from its Hebraic origins was inclined to exclusiveness, intransigence, and "proneness to resort to violence in order to impose on other people what [its] own adherents believe to be true and right."[9] (Toynbee's evolutionary account of the history of religions does not, however, exclude a theology of religion and revelation that would see God working through the evolutionary cultural processes.)

Flag waving, therefore, is an exercise in power—power that derives in significant part from these ancient sources. The New Right is bedecked with the symbols of religion and religious nationalism. Indeed, though they make distinctions—for tax purposes and for other reasons—between their work as political and as religious, they can neither distinguish nor separate the two. The United States, in fact, is in their view a sacrament of God's holy purposes. When Jerry Falwell tells us that God "established" the United States, and when Moral Majority's Tim LaHaye speaks of "our Bible-based form of government," they mean it literally, and they are speaking out of a long tradition.[10]

Jerry Falwell, Tim LaHaye, and the other prophets of the right are children of a faith tradition in this country that interpreted the United States as the new Zion. In this view, we are the promised people and this is the promised land. The tradition found characteristic expression in the last century in the work of an Ohio writer, George S. Phillips. The title of his book is quite descriptive of the content: *The American Republic and Human Liberty Foreshadowed in Scripture*.[11] Phillips's book was not creative. Indeed, as one scholar puts it: "The patent unoriginality of Phillips' book signifies its representing a major body of religious and nationalistic sentiment in the north."[12] Without a hint of hesitation, Phillips reported that God had promised in the Hebrew Scriptures to found a republic, which in remarkable detail corresponded with what Phillips saw the United States to be. Phillips' Americanism is literally divine. The United States would be the *pièce de résistance* of the Christian God. In Phillips's hands the Bible becomes stunningly prescient and precise about God's USA. The "United States of Israel," under the presidency of Moses, served in the divine plan as the prototype of the American republic. Though the ancient Hebrews lapsed into "un-American" activity and monarchy, the dream to be made incarnate in the United States was kept alive in the writings of the prophets, particularly Isaiah and Daniel, who for their "Americanism" would seem to deserve posthumous awards from the Daughters of the American Revolution. These ancient writers foretold not only the day, but even the hour of the signing of the Declaration of Independence. Isaiah 33:21 predicted in detail the Boston Tea Party, and Isaiah 49:12 foretold the coming of Chinese immigrants to California. Slavery and the Civil War were also predicted accurately. Through the work of people such as Abraham, Moses, Daniel, Paul, Luther, Calvin, Cromwell, and Wesley, the single-minded God prepared the way for the founding of a nation true to His vision. Finally it fell to the founding fathers to initiate this Christian nation, which would serve as a sacrament of the divine will for all times. Phillips's immodest conclusion: "These facts of history . . . clearly show that the Government of the United States was set up by the God of Heaven."[13]

"The worst of madmen is a saint gone mad," said the poet Alexander Pope. His reference is to the power of religiously grounded madness. And it is this that we face in the New Right. There is power in religious motivation. Religion is a response to the sacred, and the sacred by definition merits totality of response. It was the insight of Cardinal Newman that persons will die for a religious dogma who will not stir for a conclusion. If one can convincingly present one's conclusions as religious dogmas (e.g., "God is opposed to the ERA"), one's power of persuasion is immeasurably heightened. It is a sense of power more than a love of piety that fires the religiosity of the New Right.

The Power of Fear and Hatred

In a new book coauthored by Jerry Falwell and two professors from his Liberty Baptist College, we find some surprising admissions regarding the fundamentalist world. They concede that "Fundamentalists have tended to develop a kind of paranoid mentality toward the world they are trying to reach," and that fundamentalism must change so that it will "become known for what it is for, not just for what it is against."[14] That is both a major concession and a tall order. Deviant fundamentalism is animated more by what it is against than by what it is for. From its birth, fundamentalism was terrified of modernity. New ideas and approaches to religion and life, including critical reinterpretations of the Bible, terrified them. They suddenly sensed their kind of world washing away as new ideas threatened to engulf them. Even clergymen were defecting to the modernist views. "By the end of the cen-

tury," one historian has written, "it was painfully clear to fundamentalists that they were losing much of their influence and respectability." Their paranoia and antiintellectualism were "shaped
by a desire to strike back at everything modern—the higher criticism, evolutionism, the social gospel, rational criticism of any
kind."[15] Fundamentalists have tended to minimize dogmas and to
accentuate the negative in seeking unity. Even in the twelve vol-
umes called *The Fundamentals,* published between 1910 and
1915—from which the term "fundamentalist" was derived—there
is restraint in the call for dogmatic orthodoxy. The prominent fundamentalist dogma of the second coming of Jesus to reign for a
thousand years ("premillenialism") was played down in the cause
of unity. As professor George Marsden puts it: "In order to establish a respectable and self-consciously conservative coalition against
modernism, premillenial teachings were best kept in the background."[16] Fundamentalism was most notably a "conservative coalition against modernism," and doctrinal purity could be deem-
phasized in order to keep the warriors against modernism in line.
The plight of the fundamentalists has been described as akin to
that of involuntary immigrants who were being pushed into a new
and threatening world. As a result, their reaction was one of panic
and militancy. Their task was to build a fortress (subculture) from
which they could wage holy war against the menacing demons of
modernity. Such a fortress, one can imagine, would not be a
peaceful redoubt, but would be filled with fear and hatred of the
enemy, by whom they were surrounded.[17]

This horror of modernity which is at the core of the fundamentalist reaction extends from the silly to the sacred. Some fundamentalists in the 1970s railed against long sideburns, wire-rimmed
glasses and flare-bottomed pants—all of which seemed to be hippy-
inspired—hippies being the latest mode of advance men for modernism. Some churches even provided seamstresses to unflare the
pants of the Christians who were seduced into buying them.[18]

The fundamentalist camp seethes with hatred and fear. They are
against anything which even faintly threatens the old world they

are desperately trying to recreate. Tim LaHaye's book *The Battle for the Mind* is illuminating, and a fairly lurid example of the fear-hate syndrome. (Tim LaHaye is on the national board of the Moral Majority.) He is against the United Nations, which is founded on godless humanism (pp. 26–27). He is also against the public schools (p. 27 and passim), and St. Thomas Aquinas, who polluted biblical Christianity by importing pagan Aristotelian thought (pp. 29–30). He is against Michelangelo and his nude statue of David, since the Creator in Genesis told man to cover up. "Ever since," laments LaHaye, "there has been a conflict concerning clothes," with people wanting them off and God wanting them on (p. 30). He is against intellectuals and artistic geniuses because they tend to be of a melancholy temperament, which leaves them liable to atheistic, humanistic ideas and plunges them toward disorder, anguish, and despair (pp. 33–34). He is against big government, which was also caused by atheistic humanism (p. 36). He is against John Dewey, obviously, and federal aid to education (p. 45). He is against test-tube babies and B.F.Skinner (p. 82). He is against freedom for artists, lest they pander to our sensual nature (pp. 81–82). He is against Hollywood personalities, because, as he says, "Now that John Wayne has passed away," it is difficult to find Hollywood types taking strong stands on America and morality (p. 160). He is also, by the way, opposed to the ACLU, the AHA (American Humanist Association), the ECS (Ethical Culture Society), the NEA (National Education Association), SIECUS (Sex Information and Education Council of the United States), NOW (National Organization for Women) and labor unions (p. 141). He is also against the ERA which would lead, he reports, to sex-integrated restrooms, with no partitions between the toilets, male-female nude swims, even at the YMCA, and the substitution of dancing for football in physical education classes (p. 150–151). (LaHaye is quoting a series of atrocities associated with equal rights for women reported in a Concerned Women for America newsletter.) He is opposed to the Russians (p. 156) and to Norman Lear (p. 158). He is opposed to the National Association for the Advancement of Colored People and the Chicago Urban League, both formed by ethical societies, which he also opposes (p. 163). He is against the ADA (Americans for Democratic Action), and also UNESCO and UNICEF. He is very much against homosexuality, which he says is learned behavior that can be taught by homosexual teachers, particularly to prepubic children (p. 174). And finally, he is against the Department of Education (p. 211) and Jimmy Carter (p. 232).

Certainly this listing gives the flavor of life within the fundamentalist fortress. It is filled with fear and vituperation. The Russians are coming. The atheistic humanists are coming to take over our schools and communication media. The homosexuals are about to seduce our children and turn them into gays.

In spite of the absurdities inherent in this, there is also appeal here. For anyone who is upset by a rapidly changing world, the New Right gives the word that their misgivings are not for naught. To parents who feel at a distance from their children, the New Right has an answer. Their children are being seduced by alien forces in society. For people who enjoy fear—and people pay fortunes to movie theaters and amusement parks to scare the wits out of them—the New Right purveys a parade of horrors. To persons of a paranoid bent, the New Right brings assurance that they are not paranoid—people *are* out to get them. They are right to think that the nation is beset by internal and external enemies. To those who fear the "blackening" and "browning" of the United States, the New Right tells them that civil rights organizations are the products of a seditious, atheistic humanism. To men who fear the rise of women, the New Right spells out the threat to manhood that the liberation of woman presents. To those who are uneasy over the poverty that puts millions on the dole at the expense of workers, the New Right proclaims that God prospers the good and the godly. This means that the poor are neither good nor godly, and are therefore more fearsome and less deserving than we thought. To the anti-Semites who fantasize about the monetary and conspiratorial power of Jews, the New Right avers, in unguarded moments, that God doesn't like Jews either, and that they can only be saved by conversion to New Right Christianity.

Fear sells, and so does its sibling, hatred. Conspiratorial explanations and scapegoating feed our need for simplistic "sinister force" theories. As Richard Hofstadter wrote in 1963: "The recurrence of the paranoid style over a long span of time and in different places suggests that a mentality disposed to see the world in the paranoid's way may always be present in some considerable minority of the population."[19] That the "moral majority" is really a paranoid minority is not all that consoling, given the menacing power of the paranoid stream in political life, and the power of a significant minority to corrupt political discourse.

The Power of Being Partly Right

The danger from the New Right would be less if they were completely wrong. They are, in fact, responding to some important issues that have been insufficiently attended to by the rest of us. There is a lot of seductive power in the half-truth, and this power accrues to the New Right. Some people, in their zeal to rebut the crudities of the New Right, do not concede any legitimacy to their concerns. This strengthens the New Right position. It allows them to make certain issues the exclusive possession of the New Right. The rightists are addressing real problems when they speak of things like the legitimate place of religion in political and social life, the decline of family stability, the hidden value-assumptions of supposedly neutral public education, the chaotic sexual mores of the day, and issues like pornography, drug abuse, and abortion. I will turn to these matters briefly in order to show how the New Right has discovered worthy issues, and then distorted them.

Politics and Religion

One of the principal complaints of the New Rightists is that they are being criticized for doing what "liberal" religionists have always done—mixing religion and politics. They cite the work of Martin Luther King, Jr. Clearly he did not preach a privatized religion. He went from pulpit to polling booth. He took the ideals that were bred in evangelical piety and made them the basis of a movement that eventually yielded civil rights legislation and affirmative action executive orders. How dare we now complain, after cheering Martin Luther King, Jr., when another stripe of evangelicals make their own attempt to influence politics.

That objection is partly right—and partly wrong. It is correct that religion and politics do mix and have always done so. Whenever there are principles and ideals for the good and just life, we have a right to try to make them the law of the land. Many of our finest ideals, from the foundation of the nation until now, have been engendered and nourished by religious experience. They are not therefore debarred from the marketplace of political ideas, as though religion indelibly contaminated them.

Turning to the Bible for the symbols that bind us is an inveterate American penchant. On July 4, 1776, Benjamin Franklin, Thomas Jefferson, and John Adams were appointed as a committee to prepare a device for a Seal of the United States of America. It is significant that these statesmen, who were, in the words of historian-theologian Martin Marty, "in so many ways uneasy about the Jewish-Christian heritage," turned to the Bible as a first reflex.[20] Franklin advocated a design featuring Moses. In the background, the troops of Pharaoh would be seen drowning in the Red Sea. Jefferson proposed the idea of the children of Israel, led through the wilderness by a cloud by day and a pillar of fire by night. The Bible is part of the American story, and is a seedbed for the symbols of our national consciousness. It also contains ideals of social justice and peace that well merit a place in the competition of political ideas. Banning biblical ideals and principles from the political forum represents a kind of parochial secularism, as well as an innocence of American history.

On the other hand, the radical right's objections that they are just doing what King and others did is wrong. That both King and they are attempting to bring religiously affiliated ideas into politics is true. So far, so good. The issue is not whether religion has its legitimate place under the political sun. Surely it does. The question is: *how is religion being used?* To disempower and disable or to empower and enable? The former use of religion is antipolitical and subversive. People get hurt when the power of religion is thus abused. There is all the difference imaginable between what Martin Luther King, Jr., brought to the political order and what the Falwells and LaHayes bring. When King left his pulpit and ceased his political activism, many who had lacked rights before had come to possess those rights. People were voting who could not vote before, were getting hired and educated who would have known only rejection, and were finding decent housing who could not before. In short, King's interventions in politics were *enabling* and *empowering*.

However, when the Falwells of the New Right leave their pulpits and end their political activism, inasmuch as they are successful, people who had rights will have lost them. Their interventions are *disabling* and *disempowering*. Also, depending on their success, the most wholesome elements of the American dream will have been undermined. What particular groups will lose if the New Right prevails?

First of all, women. The ferocious resistance of the New Right to such matters as the Equal Rights Amendment has been telling. They claim credit for defeating it in many states, and in this case their claims may indeed be largely true. Since they defend patriarchal rights for men, equal rights for women are subversive in their worldview. If the New Right has its way, the white male monopoly that from the founding of this country has demanded and gotten a 90 to 100 percent monopoly on positions of power and prestige in church, state, business, the professions, and the academic world will continue. Affirmative action, a modest effort to ease that historic monopoly, is targeted against by the New Right. Success for them here means the further *disabling* and *disempowering* of women. To compare that achievement to that of Martin Luther King, Jr., is an obscenity.

Next, blacks will be the losers. Obviously, black women lose when the ERA loses, and all blacks are hurt when affirmative action is cut back, as the New Right and the Reagan administration is intent on doing. As I shall argue at greater length in chapter four, the New Right is racist. These, after all, are the people who started building their "Christian schools" after the Supreme Court's 1954 *Brown vs. The Board of Education* decision, which ended the "separate but equal" caste policy in the United States. (These schools have been more accurately called "segregation academies.") These New Rightists are the people who, on their checklists of political orthodoxy, never include civil rights. These are the people who, in their morally indignant writings, have no moral indignation to spare for the plight of our black brothers and sisters in this land. These are the people who resisted the civil rights legislation of the 1960s on the same grounds that they resist the ERA, saying that it is unnecessary, since the Constitution is all we need. Blacks will lose, and the second brief civil rights movement in the history of the nation will be further gutted if the New Right prevails. Again, it is an obscenity to compare this project with the work of Martin Luther King, Jr.

Poor people in general will lose as the New Right pursues its mean-spirited agenda. They have already lost as have women and blacks under the New Right policies. Hard-earned civil rights and basic human needs will be assaulted. Even legal services, without which the Constitution becomes meaningless for the legally dispossessed, will be further cut. The discussion of poverty by the New Right is befouled with strategic myths and lies. If Falwell lives in a mansion because God prospers the good, what can be said of the unprospered poor? Poverty, in the view of the New Right, is a self-inflicted wound. There are plenty of jobs for everyone, Falwell tells us. Clearly, then, the jobless don't want to work. What pity do they deserve? To cut through these lies, it is well to note some of the facts offered by a study of the Carnegie Council on Children. When you talk about the poor, to a very large extent you are talking about children.

> In 1976 . . . 25 million Americans, including 10.1 million children under eighteen, lived in households below the official poverty line, which that year was $5,815 for a non-farm family of four. Children constituted over 40% of all persons in official poverty; 15.8% of all American children that year were poor by the government's definition. But these figures understate the problem. If we use a relative definition of poverty and replace a bureaucratic definition of poverty with the American public's popular standard of half the median income, we find that more than a quarter of all American children live in poverty.[21]

Cutbacks in aid to the poor, therefore, are in great part cutbacks in aid to children. By no calculus are children poor by their own fault. Therefore, to retreat from aid to the poor to support a bigger defense budget is to prefer arms to children. Here again is the difference between a religiously motivated Martin Luther King, Jr., and the New Right. The Hebrew and Christian scriptures from which King drank are obsessed with the needs of the poor and the powerless in society. How the New Right can read those scriptures and support elitist monopolies, weaken civil rights enforcement, and cut back on aid to poor children is an epic of hypocrisy that must be called by its name.

Homosexuals too will be disempowered and insulted as the New Right gains in influence. Though the Bible contains only a handful of texts on homosexuality, the obsession with this topic in the writings of the New Right would give Freudians an analytical field day. The God of the New Right is a heterosexual God of the macho kind. Although the biblical authors do not show any awareness of homosexuality as an inborn preference, and although homosexuality in scripture has connotations of irregular cultic worship—something that has no modern counterpart—the Bible is presented as militantly antihomosexual. And, as if the Bible interpreted by the

New Right is not enough, their God even intervenes dramatically in nature to demonstrate his wrath at the very prospect of civil rights being guaranteed for homosexuals. It all happened in the summer of 1979, in Santa Clara, when the County Board of Supervisors was meeting to vote on a proposal to guarantee civil rights for homosexuals. When fundamentalist pastor Marvin Rickard rose to condemn the proposition before the board, God reacted with a sudden earthquake. The fundamentalists who were present cheered and applauded, and Pastor Marvin explained to the board that God often caused earthquakes when He was enraged at outlandish depravities in the human scene. (They never entertained the possibility that the earthquake was directed at Pastor Marvin and his followers. Neither did they advert to the discrepancy between their 10-on-the-Richter-scale reaction to homosexuality and God's meager 5.3 reaction.) Turning their backs on both the pastor and his God, as well as the earthquake, the board went on to approve the measure by a four to one vote. No retaliatory earthquakes were recorded.[22]

In other similar instances, even without the geological theatrics, the New Right has been more successful, and prejudice against homosexuals has been reinforced in many jurisdictions. Given the pedagogical power of ordinance and law, there is much cruelty in this witch hunt. It can create an atmosphere that is conducive to violence and discrimination against gays. Those who reduce the Christian religion to this kind of crusade offend not only their homosexual brothers and sisters, but also discredit the gentle religious tradition they use as a cover for their prejudice.

Beyond these particular victims of New Right politics, there are broad areas that their perverted religiosity also threatens. The outstanding "bias" of biblical Christianity is for peace (see chapter four). The New Right is wed to militarism. Being very shy of history, except as rewritten for their own purposes, the New Right does not realize how classically they represent the militaristic perversion of Christianity that began in the fourth century. At any rate, they in no way represent the Jesus who taught that he who lives by the sword will perish by the sword. The gospel, which was in its origins a force for peace, becomes in their hands a force for war.

Environmental concerns also will suffer at the hands of the New Right. The words of one of their apostles, Interior Secretary James Watt, were mentioned earlier. In a chilling way he embodies the perverted indifference to the needs of the planet earth that is part of the New Right faith. As in concerns of peace, irreversible harm can be done here if New Right influence spreads and prevails.

Finally, in this incomplete list, the cause of education will suffer. The New Right is not in favor of education. They only understand and approve of indoctrination. The so-called "Christian schools" show what the New Right would do with all education if they had the chance. Everything that promotes humanism—and almost everything but the Bible does—is banned. As one former principal of a Christian school said: "Almost all authors considered humanists—Emerson, Thoreau, even Shakespeare—are often eliminated wholesale from the curriculum at many schools."[23] Indoctrination, as opposed to education, proceeds by banning all "distracting" debate, so that a narrowness of vision is ensured. The assault on the kind of education that has always been generally esteemed in this country is proceeding, and is scoring multiple successes around the country. Here too, these people, who have moved from the pulpit to the forum of public policy, are wreaking havoc.

In response to this deceptive mischief of the radical right this may be said: convictions that are buried in pulpit and pew are irrelevant. Hitler could build a Third Reich upon the piety of Christians who kept their piety unapplied to the political order. Nevertheless, when one moves with his or her insights into the political forum, it is essential, first of all, not to distort the religion one is professing to be at least the partial basis of one's positions. This is the first failure of the radical right. They use their religious sources capriciously and erratically. (See chapter three, "The Bible as Oracle and Ouija Board".)

The second failure is that these rightists use their religious posture not only to befuddle the Internal Revenue Service, but to mask what one author has called their "meanness mania."[24] Their religion is, in spite of all their posturing, very secondary to their extreme right-wing ideology. They represent a kind of pseudoconservative elitism, which is insensitive to the poor, authoritarian, truculent, and ultimately fascistic in its spirit. That is their real agenda, and it has nothing to do with the central beliefs of the Judaeo-Christian religion they profess.

An important question arises from all of this. Why have these rightists, with their warped form of Christianity, been able to present themselves in the political order as the rightful heirs of the Christian tradition? The answer is that they saw a void and moved into it. The other Christian churches, which have the advantage of solid scholarship to put them in touch with the actual sources of Christianity, have fallen into political irrelevance. They have left the field to the moral majoritarian types. Churches that are troubled by the caricatured religion put forth by the New Right in the name of Christianity must examine their own consciences. Such an examination might lead to the following conclusions. The so-called "main-line" Protestant churches and the Roman Catholic church can be indicted for failure: they have become fixated on issues of micro-morality rather than of macro-morality and, to guarantee their own survival, they have been purveying social respectability rather than prophetic criticism.

Perhaps we can see the micromoral mentality in rudest caricature in those Christian chaplains in the German army in World War II who accompanied their troops in their ruthless invasion of the Netherlands, while *warning them against the Dutch prostitutes.* They were more concerned with illicit orgasms than with slaughter and holocaust. It is the advantage and function of caricature to show in bold relief errors that often find more subtle expression.

Some of the major Christian churches have lapsed into stubborn fixations on certain issues of private micromorality. Roman Catholicism, which has a rich tradition of social justice theory to draw from, has become overly identified with issues such as abortion and anticontraception. There is no such thing as a tidy and discrete "Catholic vote," but those politicians who are shrewd enough to move from obscurity to office usually do have a sense for the heated issues of concern in various groups. The Catholic concern has not been perceived to be militarism, racism, or environmental depredation; it has been perceived to be focused on abortion.

No one issue should be allowed to dominate the moral energies of a major church. The damage is all the greater when the position taken on the issue is absolutistic and unnuanced. Good and sensitive people and churches are divided on the abortion issue. For the Catholic Church to become identified with one position in this debate, and that the most inflexible and rigorous one, stamps that church with a harmful image. When the Moral Majority arrives with the news that God is concerned with a number of other issues, the seemingly monomaniacal Catholic voice is easily drowned out. Other churches too have shown a preference for blending piety with private propriety rather than with politics. (Had Jesus done that, he would never have been crucified.) The New Right has something to teach these churches. Biblical morality does have relevance to the macromoral order. If the major Christian churches have kept their parishes parochial, the Falwellians, at least, have come forth with the message that faith does involve politics. The good that the New Right has done by pushing religious people toward politics may already be emerging. Catholic bishops in the last year have been taking a strong position against the suicidal preparation for nuclear war that is taking place in this country and elsewhere. They have also spoken out against capital punishment and other social issues with more directness and specificity than had been their custom. They may indeed have been helped in this by the message that moral majoritarians are stamping insistently on the public mind, i.e., that religious persons will be heard from in the great debates of politics.

The desire of most evangelicals to dissociate themselves from the Falwellians and to show what they see as the true meaning of the Christian religion is another inverse benefit of the emergence of the new "Christian" right. Sheer embarrassment at what is called "Christian" these days does put those who value that term on notice to speak up.

The Family Issue

A second area in which the New Right has correctly discerned a problem is that of the needs of the family. Family life is disintegrating, with enormous human suffering resulting, and the New Right seems to be the only place where consistent concern for the family is voiced. Of course, their prescription for family stability is control by men of their wives and children. It is a macho and oppressive solution. The New Right would strip women of their sense of dignity and of their rights, make them more submissive, and in that way restore peace to the family scene. Dan Fore, former head of the Moral Majority in New York, says: "If you teach people their rights, you breed rebellion and anarchy, but if you teach people responsibility, you breed a submissive society." All this talk about equal rights for women, says Fore, "takes a woman out of her submissive role in God's line of authority and puts her into competition with the man." This is unnatural, since God has made man "the stronger vessel."[25] Their solution, obviously, is crude chauvinism.

Nevertheless, they are right that there is a crisis in the family. Their difficulty is that they miss both the causes of the problem and its possible solutions. As Rosemary Ruether says, we have to "recapture" the issue of the family. "The home is too important a place for all of us to give it away to the right." We have to recognize that the family issue is a real one, not an invention of the New Right. Again, as Rosemary Reuther says: "Spokespersons for reform need to make it clear that they have a more accurate analysis of the crises of the family than the right, an analysis that speaks more meaningfully to the real experience of ordinary people. Most women know that it is not feminism, but rising inflation, that is creating the need for the two-income family. Once in the workplace, the woman not only deals with problems of undeveloped skills, economic discrimination, and sexual harassment, but she also runs a rat race of trying to coordinate the tasks of family with those of the workplace in a system that has set the two in opposition to each other."[26]

Contrary to the thinking of the New Right, family stability cannot be legislated into being by some Family Protection Act. Poverty, inflation, joblessness, and racial prejudice are among the major causes of family disruption. These issues should be put into perspective in the family issue. The New Right knows there is a problem in family life in this country, but they do not know what the problem is or how it can be solved. They must be given credit, however, for highlighting the problem and causing excitement about it. Again, they are filling a void.

Of course, it is not true that nothing has been said or done about the family outside the New Right. Indeed, research is blossoming and conferences are proliferating on the subject, but at the level of political discourse, the family issue has been made to seem an issue of the right. What is needed is a clear-cut recognition that there is nothing conservative or reactionary about being interested in family life and its problems. Family-conscious analyses of social and economic problems will have the advantage of not seeming like a radical scheme of social engineering. What must be shown to be most in the interest of the family is for this nation to stop wasting its resources on unusable doomsday weapons, and to become, for the first time since World War II, creative and daring in the pursuit of disarmament. With so much of the economy pumped into military make-work and waste, a sick economy results, with an adverse impact on family well-being. The linking of family issues with economic and military issues is a project for all who do not wish to leave family matters, with all the emotions that are associated with them, to the New Right propaganda machine. I will treat the family politics of the New Right in chapter five, "Blueprint for a Fascist Family."

Pseudoneutrality in Public Education

The New Right is correct in recognizing that education and legislation are not morally neutral. Both embody particular moral visions of the good life. The New Right has come into a void left by a century's dalliance with the idea of "value-free objectivity." This dalliance was precipitated by the philosophy of positivism, which dreamed that one could judge things of human import without morally evaluating them. If that is hard to understand, it is only because it is nonsense.

Humans are not preprogrammed by nature in all their actions. We are, in Nietzsche's phrase, "a valuing animal." Moral values are those that concern judgment about what befits or does not befit human life and society. When we condemn rape, we are saying that that mode of sexual expression does not befit persons. If we condemn fraud, again we judge that mode of personal enrichment as unbefitting to the valuing of other persons. When we ended slavery as an American institution, it was because of a moral judgment—slow in happening—that persons cannot be treated as mercantile objects to be bought and sold, just because of the darker pigment in their skin. All judgments in the political, economic, military, or merely interpersonal spheres have a moral dimension. They have an impact on the good or ill of persons. One way or another, they affect people, in all of their preciousness, and we accordingly label them good or bad.

With the onset of positivist thinking, the basic sense of this was lost. The illusion spread that one could be truly objective only by rising above moral evaluations. Moral evaluation of course, did not cease. The mind can't turn itself off. But what did cease was candor about the fact that one was making moral judgments of a particular sort in the political, educational, and economic spheres. As a result, these moral judgments were masked and unexamined. We were just expected to accept them as amoral judgments.

Now, without showing much awareness of the positivistic illusion of value-free objectivity, the New Right has sniffed out the moral judgments all around them. The "liberals" and "secular humanists" whom they attack have their own moral agenda. Oftentimes they don't admit it. But you can't run a school and ban moral judgments at the schoolhouse door. Historically, Americans were more candid about the presence of moral judgments in the educational process. The assumption of American education up until this century was that the curriculum was awash in moral judgments, and that students should be given some courses in moral philosophy or ethics in order to be able to sort out and choose among the competing value judgments that arise in the school setting. Professor Douglas Sloan of Columbia University writes: "Throughout most of the nineteenth century, the most important course in the college curriculum was moral philosophy, taught usually by the college president, and required of all senior students. The moral philosophy course was regarded as the capstone of the curriculum. It aimed to pull together, to integrate, and to give meaning and purpose to the students' entire college experience and course of study. In so doing, it even more importantly also sought to equip the graduating seniors with the ethical sensitivity and insight needed if they were to put their newly acquired knowledge to use in ways that would benefit not only themselves and their own personal advancement, but the larger society as well."[27]

The New Right, unnourished as it is by historical studies, nevertheless knows this. They are aware that, before this century, colleges admitted that they were including moral evaluations in science, mathematics, and history, and that an effort was made to equip students to move sensitively and judiciously within the moral sphere. The New Right also knows that many of the college presidents teaching courses on moral philosophy were ordained Protestant ministers, and that this gave Protestantism some considerable moral control over the educational system and the ethics that was taught. They also know that this system came to an end. For example, "in 1895, the Amherst College catalogue devoted the entire first page of the section on 'The Course of Study' to a description of the course in ethics taught by the president of the college to the senior class. But by 1905 ethics had disappeared from its front-page billing in the catalogue, and was to be found as merely one among several courses offered in Amherst's philosophy department as an elective for sophomores."[28] The 1895 Amherst catalogue reported that "the aim of the course is, by the philosophic study of the social and political relations of the individual to his fellow citizens and to the State, to promote that moral thoughtfulness . . . which is the strongest element in true patriotism."[29] This concern for "moral thoughtfulness" as the mark of the educated person soon passed.

This rehearsal of history, as you may imagine, would set the New Right to cheering. That's all they are out to do, they would argue—"to promote that moral thoughtfulness . . . which is the strongest element in true patriotism." Here again they lapse into partial truth. The true side of their position is that there really was in the past a better understanding of the ubiquity of moral judgment, and of the relevance of the study of moral choice (ethics) for a full education. This was a healthy insight, even though the full significance of it escaped most of those involved in education in the last century. They did not, for example, spend much time pondering the moral dimension of their decision to teach history exclusively from the viewpoint of white males. That was not just a historical and educational judgment. That was a moral judgment about what befitted students and their view of morality, and about the value in history of persons who were not white males. Ethics courses that were more sensitive would have brought criticism to bear on that. Many other values of a ruggedly individualistic economics were passed on without scrutiny of what they included by way of moral presumptions. Still, the system was aware of something—something that the New Right is aware of too: schools teach more than the three Rs. Every curriculum at every level embodies moral visions and judgments. Moral judgments are made about what is to be taught and what excluded, about which values are to be accented and which demeaned. Much of this will be done implicitly, without allowing even the possibility of criticism of the operational moral values of the school system. This, in effect, is the most parochial approach to education. The moral assumptions that are operating are simply presented as coincident with reality. They may or may not be, but without an institutionalized recognition of the need for candor and systematic criticism of assumptions about moral values, the student remains uneducated about the most foundational values in the human lexicon. Fortunately, it is not only the New Right, that is beginning to see the question of moral values in education. In general education this problem is beginning to be noticed and faced. In a series of studies on the teaching of ethics in higher education, the point is being made that throughout higher education moral judgments are being ladled out, usually without criticism. For example, in a study entitled *Ethics and Engineering Curricula,* Robert Baum, himself a scientist, shows the haphazard approach to moral evaluation in engineering schools. This is no slight matter when you realize how many of our engineers move on to managerial positions and therefore control a good deal of human destiny. Baum points out that the field of engineering is and is perceived to be a "male profession." This, for starters, imparts a particular moral vision. Also, engineers are largely drawn from lower middle-class and upper lower-class people seeking upward mobility through their profession. Again, this induces attitudes that are not morally neutral. Nevertheless, the majority of engineering students have no sense of ethics as a systematic, critical approach to moral evaluation. Most of them simply assume that science and technology are concerned with factual knowledge and that moral knowledge is purely "subjective." "Since ethical knowledge is subjective and based on internal intuitions of individual persons, they believe that there is no basis whatsoever for resolving disagreements among individuals concerning ethical matters." The engineering student arrives with what Baum calls "a thoroughgoing ethical relativism." "But, paradoxically," he adds, "many engineering students are ethical absolutists, although they also share the relativists' assumption that there is no rational basis for comparing ethical positions, and they are unwilling (and/or unable) to present any arguments in defense of their own principles."

They simply assert that they are true absolutely and apply to all individuals (not just themselves). At best their position can be characterized as one of 'naive intuitionism.' . . ."[30]

It should be clear that there is more than a little similarity between the closemindedness described above and that of the New Right. Those who are naive about moral evaluation assume that their judgments "are true absolutely and apply to all individuals." This is as true of Falwellians as it is of these engineers—engineers are only used here as an example of a broader phenomenon of ignorance of ethical questions. It should also be clear how dangerous such mindsets are, since, in the case of engineers, to return to our example, we are dealing with decision makers whose judgments affect our ecology, our modes of warfare, and, in many ways, our lifestyles. Moral evaluation is dreadfully serious. And it is more than a little grim to realize that our school systems are turning out persons destined to wield significant power in our society and in our world who "are unwilling (and/or unable) to present any arguments in defense of their own principles." Therein lies the ingredients of endless disasters. Therein also lies the void that the New Right is trying to fill.

Two things are needed: first, to recognize that untested value assumptions roam about our educational settings, and secondly, to return to the wisdom of the ancient world, which knew that the study of moral-value questions was the supreme challenge to the human mind. If the chaos on the right presses us to new awareness and new policies in this area, it can only be beneficial.

The New Right at least is putting out its moral assumptions for testing, and they are learning that it hurts. Many so-called "liberals" avoid this testing because they overlook the fact that their preferred schools are not morally neutral. George Bernard Shaw has said that the essence of barbarianism is to treat one's own customs as the laws of nature. This is a barbaric temptation to which we all succumb. The New Right, in its own twisted way, is forcing a showdown on moral values, and demonstrating the need for the reestablishment of ethics as part of any sophisticated curriculum.

They, of course, would not phrase it or see it in that way, but what they do see is that those other schools are teaching ethical judgments that they do not agree with. Their solution is to abandon education in their schools and turn instead to forced indoctrination, which defeats the very purpose of schooling. Indoctrination, ironically enough, is the opposite of free enterprise in education. The rightists, who believe that God created free enterprise, do not allow it in the classroom. No competition of ideas is permitted. Robert Billings, now a top administrator in Reagan's Department of Education, in a handbook telling how to start your own Christian school, puts this warning in capital letters: "NO UNSAVED INDIVIDUALS SHOULD BE ON THE STAFF!!"[31] "Unsaved," of course, stands as the signal-word for a New Right mentality. Dissenting views need not apply. Indoctrination is not concerned with the quality of learning, but with conformity, and uniformity of results. Quality education, which opens the mind to the legitimate competition of ideas, is in fact excluded by the very principle of indoctrination. As the Reverend Rex Heath of the Mother Lode Christian School in Tuolumne City, California puts it: "When the community appeals to higher standards of academics, that always kills spiritual values. All those schools like Yale and Harvard started out as Christian schools, but then they got concerned with quality."[32] Obviously then, the New Right does not have the answer. We should credit them, however, with seeing the problem.

Moral Issues

There are other problems that they see, and their concern deserves credit. They are concerned about the proliferation of teenage pregnancy, sexual promiscuity, drug abuse, alcoholism, pornography, and abortion. It is a mistake to dismiss this as smallminded, puritanical fussing. They are genuine social problems that merit the concern of all of us—problems, however, that deserve better treatment than they receive from the radical rightists. It is one thing to say that they approach each of these issues in the wrong way; it is another thing to say these issues do not exist.

Likewise, many people see the issues, and if they see that only the New Right is addressing them with any passion, their interests and their purses go to the rightist groups.

Many people could concur with the following statement:

> Pornography destroys the privacy of sex. Parents must teach their children that sex is private and beautiful only in the marriage relationship. Pornography displays a distorted view of women. Women are shown as a masculine wish fulfillment, or many times women are depicted as being so lust-driven that they will stop at nothing to satisfy themselves. Sex is shown as a physical relationship without love; there is no true love relationship to be found here.[33]

Those are the words of Jerry Falwell. He follows with attacks on pornography, which depict the mutilation and torture of women, and with attacks on the exploitation of children in pornographic contexts. These are good things to be opposed to, and the New Right is opposed to them. They are also worried about the cult of drugs as exotic mind-exploring agents, as is many a parent. Their concern with abortion is part of a violent debate in this country that features some who seem to treat the experience of abortion as the badge of true liberation, and others who treat the first reproduction of cells as the achievement of fully fledged personhood. Neither position bears the hallmark of balance. The New Rightists are extremists and absolutists, who simplistically dismiss the complexity of the issue. But again, it is an issue that merits concern. I will attend to this in more detail in chapter five, but let it be said here that abortion is not a light issue at all. For one thing, abortion involves the use of a woman's body to solve a problem which is not only the woman's problem. The absence of men in abortion clinics, where women are normally seen accompanied by women, is an indicting fact. Except in cases of parthenogenesis, men are involved somewhere in the process. Beyond that, abortion, and especially repeated abortion, can be implicated in infertility and subsequent proclivity to premature births. This is part of the seriousness of abortion. To be at all cautious about abortion is scorned in some pseudoliberal circles. There is no sense in this attitude, and it is ultimately self-defeating. It represents another face of intolerance, and as an extremist position itself, it makes the pseudo-conservative forces look less extreme. It is quite possible, and not at all illiberal, to grant the morality of some abortions and still to be sensitive to "the problem" of abortion. Doctrinaire and unnuanced "prochoice" positions do not ultimately serve the freedom or well-being of women.

It is a laudable and wholesome exercise in humane liberalism to examine all the puritanical concerns of the New Right to find out where, amid their flaming and frantic rhetoric, a good point or two can be found. Error is a distortion of truth. It is best healed by the discovery of the truth it is molesting.

The New Right is fanatical, often ludicrous, and out of joint. But like the madman who disconcertingly sees what the sane do not, or the drunken person who blurts out truths from which the sober are hiding, they have a message for us. Not all of their concerns are chimerical. They also speak to the neglected anxieties of many people. All this translates into power.

To consolidate this power, the New Right uses an ancient tool, the Hebrew/Christian (Old Testament/New Testament) Bible. They use it to give their concerns and views divine blessing and political clout. They do this with a combination of ingenuity and presumption, and the following chapter shows how they go about it.

Chapter Three

THE BIBLE AS ORACLE
AND OUIJA BOARD

In the United States, knowing something about the Bible is a form of civil defense. The Bible, the ancient compilation of Hebrew and Christian scripture, has always been a potent source of political influence in this nation. That influence may be benign or it may be malignant. The Bible may be used in a way that promotes the needs of a just and humane society, or it may, as it does in the hands of radical rightists, become a tool for subversion. When you look at the American scene through the perverted lens of the Bible *as interpreted by the New Right,* it is a different nation that we see. If you would assess the New Right as a political reality, you must know something about their principal ideological tool, the Hebrew/Christian Bible. Learning something about the Bible does not represent a lapse from one's commitment to the separation of church and state. Rather, a basic grasp of what that book is all about is necessary to maintain that separation.

Part of the attraction of sacred books and oracles is that they promise easy and certain access to the truth. Bedeviled by the uncertainties that exist in the realms of private and public morality and politics, people are easily tempted to look for some hazard-free and divinely sanctioned source of the true and the good. The quest for an oracle is a quest for a magical source of truth that spares you the risks of human thought, dialogue, and research.

Like all magic, it offers results without proportionate causes—in this case, without dependence on real scholarship and expertise. Indeed, it gives you the grounds to disdain real learning and scholarship. These become but the vain efforts of unbelievers. Your oracle makes you an expert and lends you perfect certitude to boot. That, admittedly, is an appealing deal. It appeals to the New Right and they arrive at their certitudes through a crude manipulation of the Bible.

Sometimes we have to see the errors that are too close to us in another setting to appreciate their foolishness. A religious extravagance in the Far East shows the folly of the oracular approach to truth. There is a religion in Vietnam known as "Cao Dai." One of its most striking doctrines is that of the *corbeille à bec*. The *corbeille* is a bag with a beak-like projection. In a special liturgy, this bag is held by two members of the Law Protective Body over a board that contains the alphabet. The beaked bag, held freely over the board, tilts toward various letters. If these tiltings pick out a word, or even a verse, it is believed that this is a message from the divinity. For such messages to be valid and official, they must take place at the main temple of Tay Ninh. Here, in foreign dress, is the folly of the New Right. The Cao Dai have their *corbeille;* the New Right have their fanciful interpretation of the Bible.

How to Read a Book

To read a book you must know what kind of a book it is. Is it a factual history, or a fairy tale, a novel, or a practical instruction manual? The Bible is the book of books, and it is many things. Simplistic or uninformed handling of it is not advised.

Jerry Falwell tells us that the Bible was written by forty men over a period of 1500 years.[1] This is absurd. The Bible was written by an indeterminate number of persons and communities. It consists of multiple writings from different, and often differing, sources. Genuine biblical scholars, using the best linguistic tools and all the techniques of literary criticism, do not pretend to be completely expert in all this diverse literature. Thus, you will find biblical experts in the writings of John or Luke, or of some of the Hebrew prophets. The interpretation of ancient literature, filled as it is with untraceable references and allusions, is a major challenge. But not to the New Right. They trip through the pages of the Bible with the carefree spirit of a child on a springtime visit to the woods, adding with their imagination what their eyes do not see. One could merely laugh if all of this were not being carried out by highly financed political operatives, out to change the way we live in this country, and capitalizing on the ingrained human penchant to seek numinous auspices for personal opinions. This is precisely the project of the New Right. They use the Bible to make their opinions look like God's opinions. And they use the Bible as an ideological, political weapon.

Not surprisingly, one can find almost anything one wants in such complex literature. If you ignore the fact that the various "books" of the Bible were written in varying times for varying purposes, you can have fun playing what has come to be called the "text proof" game. So if, for example, someone who was a pacifist wanted some biblical support for his or her position, he or she could repair to Isaiah 2:4 and find it written: "They shall beat their swords into plowshares and their spears into pruning hooks." That's as clear a support for disarmament as one would like. However, the warrior lusting for battle can turn to Joel 4:10 and find this imperative: "Beat your plowshares into swords and your pruning hooks into spears." The pacifist again would be fortified by Jesus' reported words in Matthew 26:52: "Put your sword back into its place; for all who take the sword will perish by the sword." But off goes the text-proofing warrior to Luke 22:36 where he finds Jesus saying: "And let him who has no sword sell his mantle and buy one." Again, in Matthew 5:39, Jesus says: "If any one strikes you on the right cheek turn to him the other also." Nevertheless, when Jesus was struck during his trial, he did not turn the other cheek, but rather protested (John 18:22–24). And so, on and on, the text proof game is played.

Jerry Falwell's view of the Bible is unbelievably simple. "The Bible is absolutely infallible," he writes, "without error in all matters pertaining to faith and practice, as well as in areas such as geography, science, history, etc."[2] In so saying, Falwell has staked out an embarrassing position. He should be embarrassed by the obvious fact that much of the Bible simply reflects the primitive conditions of the times in which it was written.

To take the position that every verse of it is inerrant and inspired would make it difficult to explain that verse in Deuteronomy that says that a virgin who is raped must marry her attacker (Deuteronomy 22:28–29). The Bible also permits polygamy and gives rules for how to treat the children of a situation in which "a man has two wives" (Deuteronomy 21:15–17). Also, the Bible mandates more stringent measures than the Family Protection Act, with its call to reintroduce corporal punishment of children. Measured by a literal reading of the Bible, the Family Protection Act looks too lenient and indulgent. In the Bible's view, if you have a stubborn and rebellious son, who won't pay heed to his parents, and who gets into drinking and wasteful living, the parents should denounce him publicly and "then all his fellow citizens shall stone him to death" (Deuteronomy 21:18–21). Capital punishment is also prescribed for adulterous couples, and for fornicating couples if the woman is engaged (Deuteronomy 22:22–24). These are strange instructions for an absolutely infallible Bible to lay down in the name of God.

The Christian scriptures not only insist that a wife should obey her husband as though he were God (Ephesians 5:21–24), but they also portray her as naturally inferior and subordinate. The apostle Paul says that just as "Christ is the head of every man," so "Man is the head of woman." In view of this, a woman should cover her head when at prayer. "A man should certainly not cover his head, since his is the image of God and reflects God's glory; but woman is the reflection of man's glory" (I Corinthians 11:2–15). The New Right men, and the women whom they have made over in their image—women like Phyllis Schlafly, who defend the "traditional" role for women—do not blanch before the theologically argued male chauvinism of the Bible.

However, even the New Right is not out to stone rebellious children. Even they show, by what they ignore in the Bible, that the Bible requires interpretation. Interpretation, however, is a work of sorting out, of accepting and rejecting, of using literary criticism of some sort, and noting the dated or *ad hoc* quality of much that is there. The Bible says that if your eye is a cause of scandal to you, you should pluck it out (Matthew 5:29). Yet we may assume that even Jerry Falwell, were he to page through the issue of *Penthouse* that printed an interview with him, would not pluck out his eye even if he were scandalized by what he saw there.

The new religious rightists sort and pick and interpret when they read the Bible. They are not always literalists, since they in practice admit that some things must be either ignored or taken figuratively. What they do with the Bible, however, is utterly haphazard and capricious. They find whatever they want in it.

Using Falwell as an example—and remembering that he is not an original thinker, though he is surely the most visible example of deviant fundamentalism—here are some of the conclusions that are attributed to God by way of the Bible. (The references are to his *Listen, America!*) As we have seen, the free enterprise system (which for Falwell means unstricted, laissez-faire capitalism) has biblical status, since it is clearly outlined in the Book of Proverbs (p. 2). The economy should not be based on cooperative patterns, but on hard-nosed competition, because "competition in business is biblical." Ambitious and successful business management is part of what God planned for his people (p. 12). Nowhere does the Bible rebuke the bearing of armaments (p. 85). In fact, the government is assigned by God "to be a terror" to evildoers within or without this nation (p. 144). To be an effective national leader you have to be a Bible person. Nonbelievers simply could not govern (p. 17). This, of course, cuts out Jews, since not to be a Christian is to be "inherently a failure" (p. 53). Falwell bends over backwards to show his zeal for the state of Israel, but he does not hide his disdain for the status of Jews. They are "spiritually blind and desperately in need of their Messiah and Savior" (p. 98). Catholics are also disqualified for leadership, it seems, since Falwell is beside himself with grief and indignation at the election of "Comrade Mugabe" in Zimbabwe. That election, he says, may well have ended the possibility of real Christian witness in that nation. (Mugabe happens to be a committed Roman Catholic.) What is very clear is that "liberals cannot hold public office because liberals are on a path to both atheism and socialism" (p. 60). Liberals are, by definition, godless and unbiblical. The Bible also says that life begins at conception, which puts it firmly on the side of Jesse Helms and the Human Life Amendment (p. 145). God is against welfare (p. 63) because bread should come from work. "The work ethic is a biblical principle" (p. 66). The Bible, according to Falwell, also favors spanking for children (p. 121).

Tim LaHaye of Moral Majority never tires of compiling all the things that God is for and against. As LaHaye reads it, God is for these things: capital punishment, prayer in public schools, the tax-exempt status of churches, a balanced budget, reduced taxes, reduced government, and a return of the United States to the Bible, as interpreted by the New Right. God is opposed to: pornography, legalizing marijuana and prostitution, sex education, the Equal Rights Amendment, homosexuality, more federal involvement in education, busing for racial integration, and Sweden.[3]

Other members of the New Right point out that the Bible is also for the gold standard. The basis for this reading is Isaiah 1:22: "Thy silver has become dross, thy wine mixed with water." Fundamentalists have also found the Bible to be scientifically perspicacious. It was once claimed by a fundamentalist that when Job 28:25 used the expression "to make weight for the wind," it was predicting scientific findings on air pressure.

The Ouija Board

The Bible is at its best in making predictions for the New Right. Falwell notes the common doctrine of New Right religionists that the book of Revelation tells how Israel is going to be attacked by Russia. If that is frightening, fear not. The good news is supplied by chapters 38 and 39 of Ezekiel. Russia will be trounced![4]

In his 15-million copy bestseller *The Late Great Planet Earth*, to which I have alluded, Hal Lindsey finds in the Bible a detailed "countdown to Armageddon." His biblical ouija board is not much on the present, but is replete with information on the future. He gives detailed maps and all the exciting specifics of World War III. It will, of course, be a nuclear war. Ezekiel could have made a fortune on prediction, if only everything he predicted hadn't happened until thousands of years after his death. At any rate, we, through the fundamentalist Hal Lindsey, are now the beneficiaries of his seeing genius, because it is all about to happen. There, in Ezekiel's chapters 38 and 39 (also referred to with excitement by Falwell, LaHaye, and others in their retinue) is a description of nuclear war in Israel: "torrential rains and hailstone, fire and brimstone" and "a great shaking in the land of Israel," with mountains falling and cliffs collapsing and walls tumbling to the ground in the face of "every kind of terror." Ezekiel could scarcely have been referring, says Lindsey, to anything other than an exchange of tactical nuclear weapons. Lindsey even provides maps showing the route that Russia will take in its attack on Israel.

These final days before the return will have more than war to offer. All Christians will be lifted off the earth in a "rapture" to meet the returning Jesus. What will this do to the missionary effort, and where will God find forces for pressing his side of the final battle? It will be no problem. After the Christians are "raptured" up into the air, God will reveal himself in a special way to 144,000 Jews, who are going to believe in Jesus "with a vengeance." They will take off for a period of evangelism, the likes of which the earth has never known. Lindsey is rhapsodic about this. Imagine, he says, "144,000 Jewish Billy Grahams turned loose on this earth!"[5]

The chilling part of all this is that by this kind of reading of the Bible there is a real need for World War III. The final tribulation has to come. Armageddon must be realized, in all of its horror. It is a biblical necessity. One must worry when people with such fanatical beliefs get close to power. One has to hope that President Reagan had tongue in political cheek when he reportedly said during the campaign to a gathering of the Falwell faithful: "I know you can't endorse me. But . . . I want you to know that I endorse you."[6]

The approach of the deviant fundamentalists is basically a combination of magic and literalism. As with magic, numbers and mysterious formulas are given special and occult meanings. In 1922, for example, the fundamentalist *Moody Monthly* published an argument that the seven days of creation correspond in some way with the seven notes of the octave, and then related all of this to the seven sayings of Christ and the seven parts of Psalm 23. The article concluded breathlessly: "What need we of further proof that 'all Scripture is God-breathed.' "[7] Another "scholar" in the same vein developed a highly elaborate scheme that purported to demonstrate that if you were to count up all the words and letters in any given section of the Bible, the totals reached will always be in multiples of seven. The idea was well received. Another fundamentalist publication, *The King's Business,* presented this system as "An Unanswerable Proof of the Divine Authority of the Bible," which "no critic has ever dared answer." An editorial added further reassurance: ". . . while life is too short for the ordinary Bible student to attempt to go into details in following up this system, he can at least take a great deal of comfort in the discovery, and can safely rest assured that it cannot be disproven."[8]

The deviant fundamentalists are also literalists. As much as possible, they take the Bible at its word, with little, or more often no, reference to its meaning-giving context. This has a double advantage: it spares them the burden of learning what the Bible really does mean, and secondly, it preserves their idea that simple, everyday common sense is all that you need. This latter point is all-important to them, because on it rests their defense of their worldview.

Professor George Marsden points out that fundamentalism was born during a time of shifting worldviews. Fundamentalists identified with the old Baconian view of science, which put faith in common-sense observation, assuming that any normal person would see it their way. This viewpoint was challenged and widely displaced in the period from 1860 to 1925 by the view that perception always involved interpretation. Such a philosophical position, of course, called for a readiness to reassess any and all of one's preconceptions about the world and God. This was threatening. When there was added to this the new images of life that came with the industrial revolution and immigration, with their challenges to the old ways of living, the fundamentalist reliance upon common sense and straightforward intuitionism became irresistible. Evolutionism, with its notions of process and unending change, was the supreme threat. What was needed was a rock of belief that didn't change, that was not susceptible to the attack of the supposedly learned and their new-fangled ideas. That rock was the Bible.

Such a mentality has all the ingredients of a subculture, and a very defensive one at that. Since everything came to depend on their simplistic reading of Bible and of life, any contradictory ideas were the work of Satan or sick minds. From inside the subculture the emerging modern world looked insane. Those who defended the modern world were also insane. Relying on the evangelical horror of tobacco and alcohol, one early fundamentalist put it this way: "It is well known that the critics of our time have been usually men who have poisoned their nervous systems and injured their minds by the use of narcotic and other poisons."[9] Facing the question of why these poisoned minds were not all under lock and key, the same writer opined that the reason they are "not shut up in an asylum is because while their fundamental beliefs are irrational, their practical activities are sane."[10]

The biblical fundamentalists, to put it mildly, do not enter debate with respect for their opponents. Those who oppose them are either insane or immoral. Herein is a major problem that arises with the entrance of the deviant fundamentalists into the political process in a big and organized way. Political discourse in a democracy necessitates a modicum of respect operating among the participants. The alternative to this is the fascist solution, which bans opposing views. That is not the American way. It *is* the way of the New Right. Censorship is their natural reflex. Those who oppose them—the "secular humanists," in their new jargon—are corrupting the churches, our children, our schools, our government, the United Nations, and the capitalist system. The New Right can only make up a "hit list," designed to force such people out of every position of power and their books out of the libraries.

We are here at the core of how the deviant fundamentalists' use of the Bible relates to American political life. This is muddied by the "religious freedom" issue. They claim their right to participate in the political process, and such a right is incontrovertible. The question is *how* one participates, and whether one's participation will enhance or subvert that process. The point that must be made is that the New Right's use of the Bible makes them both subversives of the American way of political life and heretics to biblical religion. If this is not seen clearly, the New Right will continue to influence many with its program of subversion and repression, under a hazy claim of religious freedom and the right to participate in politics.

There are two ways in which the New Right subverts the American way of politics through its ideological usage of biblical religion: first, its principles are incompatible with pluralism; second, they are out to press their views and enforce them through a tyrannical use of majority rule and pressure tactics at various levels. I do not say that what they are doing is illegal, but I would call attention to how much subversion can be accomplished within the parameters of legality. Like communists who espouse the overthrow of the United States by force, or the American Nazi Party, which preaches the inferiority of blacks and Jews, the New Right must be allowed to speak or their rights are violated. But their kinship with other radical groups is ignored at our peril.

As to their incompatibility with pluralism, I have already stressed their oracular view of the Bible and their crude simplism, which regards disagreement with them as ungodliness or mental illness. For further illustration, let us take a closer look at their antiintellectualism, and then focus on the application of it in their efforts to reject evolutionary theory in favor of religious creationism. In that particular debate they show their full hand, and their power.

Anti-intellectualism

Fundamentalists used to be dismissed as lower-class illiterates. That never was quite true. It is not a single-class phenomenon. Fundamentalism, however, is marked by profound suspicion of the questioning mind, which is the essence of antiintellectualism, and antiintellectualism is the bane of democratic politics. It precludes the exchange of ideas and the shaping of compromises that make the system work. This fear of the learning, inquiring mind shows through the whole history of fundamentalism. It all came out in classic form during the Scopes trial. One unlettered gentleman named Joe Laffew proclaimed at an outdoor pentecostal revival during the trial: "I aint got no learnin' an' never had none. . . . Glory be to the Lamb! Some folks work their hands off'n up'n to the elbows to give their younguns education, and all they do is send their younguns to hell . . . I've got eight younguns in the cabin and three in glory, and I know they're in glory because I never learned 'em nothin." [11] A similar spirit shows up in the comment of the famed preacher, Billy Sunday: "I don't know any more about theology than a jack-rabbit knows about ping-pong, but I'm on my way to glory." [12] Sunday also said: "Thousands of college graduates are going as fast as they can straight to hell. If I had a million dollars I'd give $999,999 to the church and $1 to education. . . . When the word of God says one thing and scholarship says another, scholarship can go to hell!" [13] On a more stately plane, the same distrust of learning was expressed by William Jennings Bryan: "It is better to trust in the Rock of Ages than to know the age of the rocks; it is better for one to know that he is close to the Heavenly Father than to know how far the stars in the heavens are apart."[14]

The same spirit, in quieter dress, is found in today's Christian schools, with their indoctrinational approach to learning and their massive banning of all tainted sources of learning. These schools practice the art of the closed mind. As far as possible, minds are closed to all religious, political, social, and economic alternatives. Wheeling and dealing within the alternatives, however, is the heart of the American political system. In politics, every person is a bargainer. The fundamentalists, however, do not come as bargainers. They come as apostles, with a monopoly on the mind of God. Yielding to compromise solutions is for them defection and apostasy.

All of this comes to full bloom in the evolution/creationism controversy. For the fundamentalists, evolutionary theory is the sacrament of all that is dangerous in modernity. Again, says Bryan: "The evolutionary hypothesis is the only thing that has seriously menaced religion since the birth of Christ; and it menaces . . . civilization as well as religion."[15] Today evolutionary theory is seen as the piercing point of secular humanism and the purest expression of atheism. Anthropologist Alice Kehoe, who has studied this mindset, sums up its perspectives this way: "Evolution is change, adaptation to new circumstances. Evolutionists see a world of process, of flux, incomplete, imperfectly known. This is a world in which free-thinkers, non-conformists, adventurers can feel at home; it is not a world for the bourgeoisie. A middle-class man from a Christian background sees the world of evolution as degenerate. This is not a world in which a good husband and father would place his family."[16]

It is one thing to feel this way, to make a leap of faith to the right-wing Jesus, rally around congenial friends and preachers, and try to pretend that the world is static. That is a sectarian impulse and it is everyone's right. Its historical course has been in the direction of withdrawal from the world into an isolated subcultural haven. This is not what the New Right has in mind. It wants to turn the larger society into a subcultural haven. Therein lies the present danger.

"Scientific" Creationism

The so-called "creationist" movement shows this very danger in process. It must be remembered that this is not a private, theoretical, academic fight between these religionists and evolutionary scientists. The creationists are not just concerned with how we got here; they are concerned with what we should be allowed to do now that we are here. They are concerned about the competition of their interpretation of reality and the good life with all those other godless views. The stakes, then, are high in the creationist fracas. What they want is not just to shove a theory of origins down our throats and into our biology books, but to make Falwellian ethics the American way of life.

Historically, they have been busy at this. Thirty-seven antievolution bills were introduced in twenty states during the 1920s. The Scopes trial of 1925, in spite of how it ended, left a chill in the air regarding academic freedom and the teaching of evolutionism. The result was "a drastic cutback in serious discussion of evolution in many high school texts until it became respectable again in the 1960s."[17]

As evolutionary theory began to be restored in the textbooks, the creationists again rose in response. Professor Dean Fowler divides the fundamentalist crusade against evolution into three periods, each employing a different strategy. The first strategy, running from 1920 to 1968, was to ban evolution, and, as we have seen, it had considerable success at the textbook level. This period ended with the Epperson case, in which the U.S. Supreme Court ruled that the antievolution law of Arkansas was unconstitutional, as it proscribed a theory simply because it conflicted with a particular religious doctrine. On the basis of this, Mississippi's antievolution law was also struck down.[18] This led to strategy number two, which Fowler assigns to the 1970–1980 period. Here it was argued that evolutionism was a dogma of the religion of secular humanism, and that equal time for other religious views was necessary. This strategy also failed when tested in cases in Indiana and Tennessee.[19]

The third strategy signals the dishonesty of the whole enterprise. This strategy claims that creationism is as scientific as evolutionary theory. It seeks to mandate through law the teaching of the "scientific" theory of creationism whenever the theory of evolution is taught. As of this writing, nineteen states have creationist bills planned for the 1982 legislative sessions and creationist bills have already become law in Arkansas and Louisiana.

In the new model legislation, no reference is made to the Bible or to Genesis at all. Now, it is not equal time for differing religious views, as in strategy number two, but equal time for differing scientific views. This strategy, it is hoped, will withstand the tests in court. Of course, writers of the New Right still admit that their position is based on religious faith. Tim LaHaye admits that accepting creation as the direct activity of God "has always been a matter of faith in the revelation of God."[20] He declares it obvious that anyone who does not believe in a supernatural God would find it hard to accept creation. He then goes on to say that it is getting easier today because creationists are finding lots of scientific faults in the evolutionist theory and lots of evidence for their own.[21] To this effect he quotes a Dr. Henry M. Morris, who is known as "Mr. Creation," and who founded the Institute for Creation Research. Note, then, that LaHaye admits Creation is a religious dogma, now allegedly being supplemented by scientific discovery. This only makes it "easier" to believe; it does not constitute the grounds for the belief, which are, of course, faith in a supernatural God who made the world in six days.

The third-stage campaign, in Fowler's format, is well under way, and he predicts a much more vigorous prosecution of their goals. Aside from the development of bills that will try to make it look as though two scientific views were engaged in fair competition, state initiatives and local referendums will also be attempted. Creationists in Oregon have already begun collecting signatures to this end. Another tactic that is under way is pressure on local school boards to develop "balanced" treatment of creationism and evolution. A number of school districts already have this "balanced" approach in place. These include Dallas, Texas; Fayette County, Kentucky; Phoenix–Talent School District, Oregon; Columbus, Ohio; Kanasha County, West Virginia; and Racine, Wisconsin. School boards in Florida and Michigan are also experiencing more pressure for implementing creationist indoctrination. Efforts will also be made to develop new creationist textbooks and to bring about a de-emphasis of evolution in standard biology textbooks.[22]

The New Right, then, is not content to preach creationism in fundamentalist churches and schools. They want to give this eccentric religious view official status, alongside scientific studies of the development of species. Actually they do not really want the "balanced" treatment, because in their view evolutionary theory is the work of the anti-Christ, and they are not comfortable about having equal time with the anti-Christ. Thus, the pressure tactics on school boards and, even more important, the effort to repress treatment of evolution in standard texts, reveals their real agenda. Their goal is the suppression of godless humanism in the form of evolutionism. As LaHaye says, the answer to how life got here is found in the first verse of the Bible, in Genesis 1:1. Then, he says, the details of that creation are found in Genesis 2:1–7, and those details indicate an instantaneous act of God, not any drawn-out natural process.[23]

Among those who reverence the Hebrew/Christian Bible, only a small literalistic minority believe that the authors of Genesis were in a position to dispute the evolutionary findings of modern science regarding the development of species. The texts in question were concerned with stressing the religious conviction that God is the ultimate source of all that is, and that all of nature is dependent on God's undergirding creative presence. The Roman Catholic *Jerusalem Bible* includes a note on the creation story saying that "it would be a mistake to seek points of agreement between this schematic presentation and the data of modern science. . . ."[24] The note adds that the creation account is "deliberately fitted into the framework of a week, which closes with the sabbath day of rest." Inasmuch as the imagery of the account is related in any way to science, the note explains: "The text makes use of the primitive science of its day."[25] The authors of Genesis were concerned to state that God was the Creator, and the source of all that is. It was not their purpose to write a scientific treatise on how creation unfolded.

The authors of the book of Genesis move freely with their images. The creation passage in Genesis is ascribed to what is known as the "priestly source," and so their literary choice to divide the process up into a seven-day week allowed them to put in a priestly plug for the Sabbath—since even God is presented as observing the Jewish Sabbath. The free-moving symbolism of the account is also signaled by such things as the creation of day and night on the first day and no sun or moon being created until the fourth day. Scientific consistency was not the point; religious symbolism and faith were the issues for the authors of Genesis. Most Christians and Jews who accept this text as scripture have no problem linking it with evolutionary theory. Indeed, it is commonly held that evolutionary data enhance the sense of the divine creative genius rather than disparage it. There is nothing in evolutionary science that threatens the religious message of God's creative sovereignty found in the Genesis account.

When the New Right call their bizarre distortion of Genesis "science," as is their current strategy, to force their views into our schools and textbooks, the word *fraud* is applicable. Their contorted reading of Genesis is not science; it is not even good Bible reading. As scientist Niles Eldredge puts it: "Creationism isn't science. . . . Science is the enterprise of comparing alternative ideas about what the cosmos is, how it works, and how it came to be. Some ideas are better than others, and the criterion for judging which are better is simply the relative power of different ideas to fit our observations. The goal is greater understanding of the natural universe. The method consists of constantly challenging received ideas, modifying them, or, best of all, replacing them with better ones."[26]

Nothing could be less suited to the oracular mentality of the deviant fundamentalists. The Creation Research Society, which is intended to give an aura of science to the creationist faith, consists of six hundred members. LaHaye tells us that membership in the society is limited to "men who hold graduate degrees in science and have signed a statement of their belief in creation."[27] Their conclusions, in other words, precede their research. That is not science—or research. What is involved here is the misuse of the Bible, and the attempt to legislate the results of that misuse on the larger society.

If we are going to let creationism pass as a science deserving equal time in our educational system, then we have to be even more democratic than that. There are other theories on the origins of life on earth. Some argue that we were "seeded" by another civilization from an advanced species on another planet. Make room in the science books for that. Also, the Jewish creation story is not the only religious account of our origins. In one ancient creation myth, Eurynome, the Goddess of All Things, assumed the form of a dove and laid the Universal Egg from which all things hatched. Should not goddess theories of egg-laying creation be granted equal time? Surely if some feminists wanted to open a Goddess of All Things Creation Institute, they could produce enough evidence of ovulatory production in the whole biological order to give "scientific" appearances to their egg hypothesis. Their case would be as good as that of the creationists today, and would give a nice egalitarian touch, since our history has been so taken up with myths of creation by a male god. The Goddess too deserves her day. And so it can go on, and on.

The scientific teaching on evolution is not the product of a mystical reading of some sacred text. It is not traceable to some oracular utterance in the religion of some sect. It resulted from observation of the interrelatedness of all life and from growing evidence of change and development in life forms. So massive a theory allows for disagreements on many points regarding *how* evolution took place. The creationists leap on any such disagreements as a sign that the theory is coming apart. In fact, it is not. For one hundred years the biological sciences have found that the basic assumption of evolutionary theory, i.e., that there is one fundamental scheme of interlocking similarities in all of life, endures. Evolution may be considered "only a theory" if you allow that it is the only theory available. That the process took place is supported by massive and increasing evidence. How it took place, in leaps and bounds or in an orthogenetic line, is debated. As the Jesuit priest and scholar Teilhard de Chardin said, evolution is "a general condition to which all theories, all hypotheses, all systems must bow and which they must henceforward satisfy if they are to be thinkable and true."[28]

Science has much to learn about the process, but the process keeps revealing itself. When the oracles arrive on the scene with their six-day creation hypothesis and call it science, their claim is groundless. The absurdity of that claim has to be repeatedly exposed as they attempt to undermine both education and civil liberties with their creationist crusade. In 1923, fundamentalist Frank Norris said: "Evolution is Bolshevism. . . . It eliminates the idea of a personal God, and with that goes all authority in government, all law and order."[29] Such nonsense is still the stuff of today's creationism. It insults both science and religion.

Reclaiming the Bible

The New Right offends the Bible as well as the flag. To counter them it is necessary to have a basic sense of what the Bible is and how the New Right is at odds with it. Since they claim that their views are utterly Bible-based, we can't ignore the Bible in dealing with them. This is distasteful to many Americans, but then civil defense is often distasteful, at best.

The hesitancy to get in touch with the Bible is understandable in the American tradition, since it seems that we are being made to argue like theocrats rather than democratic citizens. This hesitancy must be overcome. The Bible is not just something you find in your motel drawer; it is a force in politics. Strangely, we would assume that we cannot study politics in Eastern or Middle Eastern countries without knowing their Sutra scriptures or their Koran. Yet the assumption has reigned in American politics that the Bible is negligible in our political debate. Meanwhile, aberrant readings of the Bible are attempting to work their way into law, and affect the rights of persons in areas such as education, reproduction, and basic civil liberties.

I have been quoting liberally from New Right biblical devotees. To introduce my short lesson on the actual meaning of the Bible, it might be well to hear from two old-time Baptist preachers who wrote to Jerry Falwell. They were bred on the same Bible as Rev. Falwell, but they emerged from it with a very different spirit. Here is the letter to Pastor Falwell from two of his Baptist brothers.

> *Dear Brother Falwell,*
>   We are replying to your "Moral Majority" Questionnaire recently received. We are two ordained Baptist ministers, both graduates of the Southern Baptist Seminary. Gordon Poteat graduated from Furman University, B.A. 1910, and Wake Forest College, M.A., 1911. Lilburn Moseley graduated from Wake Forest College, B.A. 1926. From 1919 to 1937 Poteat was a Baptist missionary in China, most of that time teaching Christian Ethic courses to Chinese students in Shanghai Baptist College, later named the University of Shanghai. Returning to the U.S. in 1937, he taught seminary and university students. For thirty three years Moseley was a minister of Baptist churches in four states.
>   As to abortion, you have the right to hold to your position and are free to propagate it. It is another matter when you seek to have a federal law which would deny women the right to control their bodies and decide whether they would bear children. You would make such a choice a felony with criminal penalties. When men brought a woman taken in adultery to Jesus they had the Bible on their side in demanding that she be stoned. (They didn't bring the

man involved.) Jesus was more compassionate. He did not condemn her. He forgave her.

You announce that you are opening an office in Washington. When you are there, you say that you will divest yourself of your role as a minister of the Gospel and assume a purely political role. This is easier said than done. For example, one of your goals is the passage of a law which will qualify a fertilized ovum as a human being with constitutional rights. You want to legally impose on all women criminal penalties for disobedience despite widespread disagreement among most M.D.s and ministers of the Gospel. This savors of a return to the state church of Virginia which had a law making it a felony to deny the Trinity and putting Baptist ministers in prison for preaching without a state license. We thought this had been outlawed for good in the United States after Jefferson and Madison secured the abolition of all state churches in the Colonies, leading to the First Amendment to the Constitution.

You object to the United State Senate's decision to return to Panama the land seized by T.R.Roosevelt. It was the kind of treaty which the great powers of that time imposed on weaker people. Instead of this impressing you as an act of justice enhancing the prestige of the U.S. in all South America, and giving evidence of "moral" integrity, you look upon it as "weakness."

We are troubled by the way you quote isolated passages of scripture, without regard for context or historical background, to serve your purpose, while ignoring more relevant passages which oppose your point of view. We refer to your support of greater and greater military power, when it was Jesus who said, "Put your sword back into its place; for all who take the sword will perish by the sword." (Matt. 26:52). With Roman soldiers on guard in every city in Jesus' homeland, he said "Love your enemies . . ." (Matt. 5:44). Paul knew what Jesus taught. "If your enemy is hungry, feed him . . ." (Romans 12:20). Dr. Falwell, you seem to say, "If your enemy opposes you, bomb him." Doesn't Christianity have anything to say about reconciliation, forgiveness, the "second mile"? Preachers don't need to encourage a race in armaments, leading to atomic annihilation. Leave that to those for whom life is cheap, and Jesus' way is ridiculed as impractical. We would like to see you with those who "beat their swords into ploughshares, and their spears into pruning hooks." (Micah 4:3). You appear to have a crusading concern for the fetus, little consideration for the millions of people who would perish in an atomic war. You, like the rest of us, believe not so much what you profess but what you practice. Informed opinion does not doubt that the U.S. can kill every thing that lives in the Soviet Union. They have the power to do the same to us. Eisenhower's fear of a military-industrial complex is now a reality. Why then do you advocate more bombs for our enemies and less bread for our poor? In support of your position you quoted these words of Paul, "Let every one be subject unto the higher powers. For there is no power but of God; the powers that be are ordained of God." (Romans 13:1) Paul was referring to Rome. You apply it to the United States. Why not apply it to the Soviet Union or to Communist China? This would line up "Christians" behind every iniquitous government. The fact is that Paul, with hundreds of the followers of Jesus, refused to worship the emperor and lost his life. A literal interpretation of an "inerrant and infallible" Bible would reduce Jesus to a least common denominator leaving him without unique authority as God's Son and our Master.

We are concerned about the moral conditions of our country, as you are. We must repudiate the methods you would use in correcting these conditions. You have the opportunity to speak for the poor, the ostracized, the handicapped, the sinful, the voiceless, even as Jesus did. We regret that you seem to line up with the powerful, the militarists, the advocates of "superiority." We would like to see you become the "servant of all," a "peace maker," practicing a "morality" above reproach, and forgiving and loving those who fall below your standard. Your appeal for money seems to be based on fear. Your symbol is political. Your methods are punitive. How do you reconcile your philosophy with the teachings of Jesus, your program with the Kingdom of God?

> Fraternally,
> Gordon Poteat
> Lilburn Moseley [30]

Thus far the words of the pastors. That leaves us with the question: will the real biblical people stand up? Who is using the Bible correctly? Pastor Falwell? Or Pastors Poteat and Moseley?

The Bible without Magic

The Bible, the "good book" as it has been fondly called, is not all good. That is the first lesson for Bible readers, whether they read it for religious purposes or to examine its political import as a document of considerable power in the affairs of this nation. There is in the Bible darkness as well as light, and considerable darkness at that. To a great extent the Bible simply records the lifestyles and politics of other times, with all their iniquity, primitivism, and chicanery. Pious efforts to portray all the worthies of the Bible as respectable, if not saintly persons, are in vain. King David, by any definition, was a hoodlum king. Sending off Bathsheba's poor husband on an impossible, charge-of-the-light-brigade-type military adventure so that he could claim the attractive widow for himself, is perhaps David's best-known atrocity, but it does not exhaust his repertoire. The Bible presents slavery, bigotry, and truculent bellicosity without negative judgment. Jesus is presented as speaking of slavery without ado or condemnation. The epistles of the Christian version of the Bible speak of the obligations of slaves to their masters, without condemning the institution of slavery.

Parts of the Bible were banned in the past as reading in Catholic convents because of their exuberant portrayal of sexuality. The faithful have managed to turn a discreet eye from the unpleasant or outrightly sordid parts of biblical accounts, or to explain them away with exegetical wizardry as symbolic of some edifying good. No such contortions are necessary. What is needed is simply an awareness that to a great extent the Bible is reportorial. It describes the existent mores of another day. Sins were recorded along with virtues. If this is true, why all the pious fuss about the Bible? Why does this book incense or induce reverence? The answer is that the Bible is not all darkness. It contains light and inspiration that have affected large portions of the world's populations throughout history. Amid the darkness of the Bible there emerges a vision of what human life could be, were we to be gathered together in justice and peace. The picture of God that emerges in the Bible is a God with moral and political intentions. God is presented as intent upon seeing this recalcitrant creation of His turn *from* patterns of war, domination, enslavement, and alienation *to* patterns of peace, reconciliation, justice, and cooperation. From the perspective of God, hostile divisions are inimical to a flourishing humanity. In God's eye-view, says the Bible, "there are no more distinctions between Jew and Greek, slave and free, male and female," since all of us are "one" (Galatians 3:28). This core vision of the Bible is not at all sectarian. Its appeal is to *humanitas* and to the goods that enhance us all. It is the core vision that Bible reading seeks.

The problem, therefore, is one of criteria. How do you distinguish the light from the darkness in the Bible? There are, in effect, two Gods in that complicated book—one that seems at home with devastating evils that even our partially civilized world has repudiated, and another God who has a better idea.

Four basic rules can help with Bible interpretation. First, distinguish between the Bible as *descriptive* and the Bible as *prescriptive*. Sometimes the Bible is merely describing the rules and customs of the time in which it was written. At such times the Bible may simply be reflecting the militarism, sexism, and general barbarity of the day. The biblical writers are giving us history, but not much by way of edification.

Second, distinguish ad hoc judgments from those that have a potentially broader application. Thus, if Paul suggests that the unmarried should not marry because Jesus would be coming back soon, thus leaving too little time for all that marriage entails, he was making an ad hoc judgment that was also erroneous (I Corinthians 7:25–31). His position may be of interest, but is clearly not relevant advice, and should not be used to promote celibacy today. When the ancient Onan is condemned for spilling his seed, it is not a big problem to see the ad hoc nature of his indiscretion. He was being presented as a violator of the levirate law that commanded a brother to have children with his dead brother's wife if the brother died without issue. Onan accepted having intercourse, but not the consequences of it, and the Bible records a dim view of his action. (He was struck dead for his incomplete cooperation [Genesis 38:6–10].) This particular incident had some interest for a polygamous society that wanted no man to die without progeny being attributed to him. It has no relevance to modern discussions of birth control or masturbation, though it has been applied to both. Also, the early Christian community is presented as communistic in its lifestyle—something we never hear about from the Falwellians. "The faithful all lived together and owned everything in common; they sold their goods and possessions and shared out the proceeds among themselves according to what each one needed" (Acts 2:44–45). This was suitable for their situation and spirit. It is not entirely ad hoc in its meaning since it suggests a certain limit to the instinct of private property which has a broader relevance. It also suggests the centrality of sharing and responding to the essential needs of all. Still, it does not suggest that 100 percent common ownership is a mandatory formula for all times and civilizations.

Third, distinguish the leitmotifs from chance themes. If certain themes recur with great frequency in the Bible, there is a good chance that they represent a core message in the biblical tradition. If such leitmotifs are not merely descriptive, but are prescriptive of a new way of life—such as is the case with the biblical notion of justice—then we are dealing with the central, and not the incidental, biblical message.

Fourth, in case of doubt—and doubt there will always be in the interpretation of any literature—apply the criteria of fruitfulness and coherence. To get to the central normative message of the Bible, doubt may be resolved in favor of that which promotes and promises coherent and fruitful expression of the human good. The Bible is most relevant in those of its teachings which are most likely to help human life to survive and thrive.

Permit me to apply these four rules, briefly, to what may be the most insistent theme of the Bible—its teachings on justice. It is illuminating that justice, so strikingly important in the Bible, is such a neglected Cinderella for the Falwellians. Their silence on social justice is the Achilles' heel of their claim to biblical status.

The Bible's Justice

Justice can stake out a claim to being *the* major leitmotif of the Bible. A distinctive theory of justice flows through the entire Bible. You do not, of course, find in the Bible a formal treatise on justice in the modern vein. Nevertheless, as Professor Stephen Charles Mott puts it: "There is a unified picture of justice which appears throughout the Bible and in a great variety of literary forms."[31]

In the Bible, justice is, first of all, a principal attribute and passion of God. It is more than just another value in scripture; it is seen as God's stake in history. Isaiah asks in what sense God is holy and the answer is that God's holiness is shown by God's justice (Isaiah 5:16). God is a "lover of justice" (Psalm 99:4). If you want to boast, Jeremiah says, boast of knowing God, and to know God means to know God's justice (Jeremiah 9:24). If you would love me, says the biblical God, love and do justice. Doing justice is communion with God. Jesus says that if you bring your gift to the altar with great piety and become aware that you have not done the reconciling work of justice, you are to leave the holy place, attend to the work of justice, and then you are qualified to return to worship (Matthew 3:23–24). Liturgy without a lived pattern of justice does not qualify as worship.

So what then is this justice upon which God puts so high a stake? For one thing it is utterly un-American in its concept. Our concept of justice is that of a blindfolded woman holding a scale that is perfectly balanced. The Bible would have none of that. Biblical justice would tear off that blindfold and check to see who is messing with the scale. Sure enough, it would be quickly discovered that the scales do not balance, that there is an unfair tilt toward the well-off and the powerful. As Professor Norman Snaith says of biblical justice: "Here is no justice, blindfoldedly holding the scales in just equality. She watches for the rich . . . and throws in her sword against them."[32]

Biblical justice is, in a word, worldly-wise. It acknowledges that in the real world of humankind justice is harder for some to come by than for others. Hence, the imagery of justice in the Bible is more dynamic and concrete than the abstractness of the balanced scales. Justice is more like a mighty mountain stream, tumbling down a ravine with enormous power, taking all that it touches with it. Justice should roll like the waters of a perennial stream (Amos 5:23). And the goal of this thundering torrent that God wants justice to be is not at all a modest one. It is "to deliver all the oppressed of the earth" (Psalm 76:9). In short, the goal of justice is the utter elimination of poverty and oppression from this earth. God's mandate is blunt: "There shall be no poor among you!" (Deuteronomy 15:4)

The Bible makes no distinction between the deserving and the undeserving poor, between the needy and the "truly needy," as we hear the term today. Poverty, as such, is repugnant to justice, because "the poverty of the poor is their ruin" (Proverbs 10:15). And the flesh of the poor is too precious in God's eyes to bear the blight of ruinous poverty (Psalm 71:12–14).

That is another striking feature of biblical justice: it has a bias toward the poor. As one biblical scholar puts it: "There is a deep-seated and fundamental bias at the root" when you come to biblical justice. This bias is "a special consideration for the poor and the downtrodden. It crops up again and again." The principal Hebrew word for justice "has from the first a bias toward the poor and the needy." [33]

With seemingly disconcerting imbalance, the biblical God looks at the destitute in society, the failures, the convicted prisoners, the dropouts, and those whom Dickens called "the unsoaped" and says: "Blessed are you." Then God looks at the secure and respectable people and says: "Woe to you. It would be easier to get a camel through the eye of a needle than to get you to understand that justice which is to be the mark of the reign of God" (Matthew 19:24; Luke 6:20–26). The conclusion of all of this is not that the secure should become poor, since "there shall be no poor among you." Rather it directs people to view reality with the eyes of the poor, to think from the standpoint of the plight of the powerless poor, and then to do justice of the sort that will sweep away all poverty with the roar of a gushing stream. In the Bible, the burden of proof is not on the poor to explain their condition, but on the rich for permitting and profiting from poverty.

There is a final attribute of biblical justice—its concern with redistribution. As Professor Mott says: "The scriptures do not allow acceptance of a condition where groups or individuals are denied the ability to participate fully and equally in the life of the society."[34] Biblical justice, in short, treats everyone in accordance with their worth and their needs—not just in accordance with their earned desserts and merits. "If your brother becomes poor and his power slips, you shall make him strong" (Leviticus 25:35). His problem becomes your problem. In the institution of the Jubilee Year this comes out most clearly. The Jubilee Year occurred every fifty years. If I were a ne'er-do-well farmer who fell into great debt and sold my farm to you at an exorbitant price, come the Jubilee Year, I have the farm back and you lost all claim to it. This comes off as rather socialist, to say the least, but the idea of it was simply that "there shall be no poor among you" and that extends even to ne'er-do-well farmers. Their lives too are precious in the sight of God. Also, in the Jubilee Year, all debts were to be cancelled.

The institution of the Jubilee Year seemed to have arisen out of the insight that wherever there is immoderate wealth and immoderate poverty, there is no justice. Even if all dealings were scrupulously fair during a fifty-year period—which has never happened—there would still be the need for gross redistribution at the end of that time. Some people are pluckier than others, or luckier, which is the usual route to wealth. Some people are smarter and more industrious, but whatever the reason is, poverty and wealth come to coexist in society unless one does something about it. The Jubilee Year, by redistributing wealth, was one response.

Of course, the Jubilee Year was not always honored. Wealth has its ways. It was however, recorded in books and in the Bible, and it did enshrine an ideal of biblical justice—that society should be so arranged that "there shall be no poor among you." What is especially interesting about the Jubilee Year for Christians today is that recent scholarship is stressing that Jesus was proclaiming the Jubilee spirit as his own, e.g., his proclamation that his coming was "the acceptable year of the Lord," and his urging the forgiveness of debts. (There is no indication that Jesus was a "supply-sider.")

This, then, is the way of biblical justice, from the Hebrew through the Christian scriptures. This is how it fares with the four criteria I suggested. First of all, it is prescriptive, pointing out a new way of living and sharing. It wasn't merely describing how people actually lived, because people never have lived that way with any consistency. In regard to the second and third criteria, justice is not an ad hoc, episodic theme in scripture, but thoroughly pervades it, climaxing in the figure of Jesus, who was perceived to be a prophet of biblical justice. Fourthly, it contains a generous spirit that could be incarnated in various systems of government that would be primarily concerned with the least powerful in society. Biblical justice is a notion that would condemn the excesses of both capitalism and socialism, pointing always to more creative ways of sharing and living, and thus ending the two greatest expenses in any society—poverty and conflict.

Strange indeed that this grand theme of the Bible is so little noticed by the New Right prophets. They are fixated upon biblical side issues, such as homosexuality, and are never tired of pointing out how God destroyed Sodom and Gomorrah because of it. Here again, they are unbiblical. They ignore, for example, Ezekiel on the Sodom affair: "Behold, this was the guilt of your sister Sodom: she and her daughters had pride, surfeit of food, and prosperous ease, but did not aid the poor and the needy" (Ezekiel 16:49). As theologian Robert McAfee Brown observes: "The notion that destruction might come to those with a 'surfeit of food and prosperous ease' who 'do not aid the poor and needy' never comes into Falwell's purview."[35]

In place of a concept of social justice, such as the Bible insists on, Falwellians prefer gestures of compassion. Thus Falwell makes periodic pitches for aid to Cambodian refugees in Thailand. However, this merely covers up the real issue. As William Fore of the National Council of Churches says: "The emphasis on relief masks the basic courses of world hunger and the economic displacement which benefits the U.S. at the expense of the Third World. Falwell's philanthropy combines genuine pity with a veiled display of power, and an implied claim to superiority which neatly obscures the deeper issues of justice and judgment."[36] It is in the interest of the comfortable to leave unjust systems intact and only make gestures to the victims of those systems. This is the opposite of the biblical approach. The poor deserve help not out of a condescending benevolence or mere compassion, but strictly out of justice— justice that must breach the offending structures and arrangements that keep the poor in their poverty.

Conclusions on the Bible

The Bible is a compilation of some of the principal documents of the Jewish and Christian religions. It is not a magical book. Its authors did not have any foreknowledge of events. Indeed, as with Paul, who expected a second coming of Jesus in his time, the authors did not even have powers of prediction for their own days. The tendency of deviant fundamentalism to use the Bible fancifully, as a predictor of events in our day and beyond, is a classical indulgence in magic. It is commonly used by the New Right as a front for extremist right-wing ideology. The New Right clearly is entitled to enter the political process under our system. The appropriate response to them is not suppression, but criticism. That criticism has to extend to their use of the Bible as a political tool.

There are many ways in which the Bible can be used. Religious persons in the Jewish and Christian traditions find in the light of scripture intimations of a divine gift. Without any recourse to magic or oracular voodooism, they feel from their religious experience that the sublime message of this ancient text bears the imprint of the divine. In this spirit, they would label some parts of the Bible "revelation," and they use these scriptures to nourish their sense of God and their commitment to justice and peace on this earth. Such Christians and Jews make good neighbors and good citizens. They have every reason to rise in criticism of those rightists who manipulate the Bible for purposes that are clearly subversive. Fortunately, many of them are doing so. A statement by fifteen American church bodies criticizing the radical right condemned their oracular and magical use of the Bible. The signatories said: "On theological and ethical grounds, we reject the assumption that human beings can know with absolute certainty the will of God on particular public policy issues. Many in the religious right seem to have forgotten the clear Biblical witness and central Christian acknowledgment that all of us are finite, fallible, and sinful. They make claims to knowledge of God's will for our nation that no Christian is entitled to make. God wills peace, justice and liberation for all His children. . . . We are to love God with all that we are; we are to love our neighbors as ourselves; we are to do justice, love mercy, and walk humbly with our God. But we who are finite and fallible cannot claim to know with certainty the appropriate response to God's requirements at a particular moment in history."[37]

Donald W. Shriver, president of Union Theological Seminary in New York City, directs the New Right to heed the plea of Oliver Cromwell: "I beseech you, by the mercies of Christ, think that you may be wrong!" Shriver points to the political danger of the magical, oracular certainties of the right and calls for the "political virtue" of humility. He recalls Judge Hand's dictum: "The Spirit of Liberty is the spirit that is not too sure it is right."[38] The Spirit of Liberty is the American spirit, which the New Right lacks.

Chapter Four

THE AMNESIA
OF THE NEW RIGHT

The amnesiac illustrates the importance of the past. He does not know who he is because he does not know his personal history. Without a consciousness of history, one's actual identity is lost to one. This is a state in which all of us, to some degree, find ourselves. And this clearly is the state in which the denizens of the New Right find themselves. They do not know where they came from and therefore they do not know who they are. Their dabbling in history is always fanciful—like the amnesiac who, not knowing whence he comes, has decided to make things up to pass himself off as whatever he now purports to be. For example, the New Right never tires of telling us that this nation was founded by Christian men explicitly relying on the Bible. The myth then continues, saying that we have fallen away from our Christian origins and are being called and legislated back into them by the New Right. In historical fact, the churches were never weaker than at the founding of the nation. Historians estimate that somewhere between 4 and 7 percent of the first American citizens were formally church members.[1] Failure to be an active church member was no liability at all. As historian Martin Marty writes: "Thomas Jefferson, James Madison, George Washington, Benjamin Franklin, and most of their colleagues and peers were quite discontented with orthodox Protestant teaching and practices."[2] Their flirtation with deism and other European imports was not seen as any kind of political limitation, though they would all have been written off as "secular humanists" by today's religious right. These facts do not affect the New Right in their imaginative accounting of our biblical, Christian origins.

Members of the New Right are afflicted with other, more serious forms of amnesia. It is not just their magical misuse of the Bible that distorts their vision. Their consciousness is also bastardized by an unawareness of who their parents are. On the crucial political issue of war and peace, though they know it not, they are the children of Constantine and of the warring marauders of the Crusades. When it comes to peace, they belong to the illegitimate Christian line. History would tell them this but they do not pay any heed.

The New Right claims to represent Christianity and the Bible. They see themselves as the pro-Bible, pro-Christian, and promoral faction of our citizenry. What they do not realize is that Christianity is not just a product of a book; it is also a force in history. The biblical message, historically conditioned itself, was taken up into the swirl of history, with all its struggles and machinations. When you use the word "Christian," you import a whole *history* of meanings. The Bible did not flow like an unpolluted stream through time. This thing called Christianity has had a wild history—some of it marvelously inspirational, some of it a perfect horror. When someone claims to represent Christianity, we must demand to know whether it is the horror or the inspiration they represent. When someone wants to apply "Christianity" to the critical issues of war and peace, at a time when war can end life on this planet, we must be particularly attentive to what they are offering us.

It is a fact that the Bible was much concerned with issues of war and peace. It is also a fact that the family of peace-related ideas in the Bible picked up a lot of unsavory relatives as it moved through history. What we want to know of the New Right, then, is which part of the clan of historical Christian ideas they represent.

To find out, let us briefly review the travails of Christianity in its encounters with the issues of war and peace. I will point out the New Right's relationship to the consecration of violence by decadent Christianity, and then examine in more detail the millenarian need for war to which I have already referred. Next, we can look to the historical Christian forms of anti-Semitism, racism, and anti-Catholicism, and see how they are reflected in the "Christians" of the New Right.

From Christ to Wotan

Peace is another of the crowning leitmotifs of the Hebrew/Christian Bible. Peace was central to the teaching of the Hebrew prophets. The vision of what life would be when God achieved his blessed rule over our belligerent world was a vision of *shalom*, of peace. All manifestations of violence and hostility would dissolve in the peace that must come about. "They will do no hurt, no harm, on all my holy mountain" (Isaiah 11:9). The lion will lie down with the lamb. "Nation will not lift sword against nation, there will be no more training for war" (Isaiah 2:4). They will "hammer their swords into ploughshares, their spears into sickles" (Isaiah 2:4). Even the text from Joel, "Hammer your ploughshares into swords, your sickles into spears" (Joel 4:10), which I cited earlier as an example of the text-proof game, is spoken in irony to the nations who will not heed the call of God to peace. They will, as a result, founder in war. The consistent message is that peace is God's way, and when God gets his way there will be peace. The goal and essence of the "reign of God" is a "peace that has no end" (Isaiah 9:7).

The early Christians had no doubt at all about how to interpret the Bible in this regard. God is called the "God of peace" (Hebrews 13:20). They used the word "peace" to greet one another and it was also their favored word in epitaphs. To say that persons had died "in peace" (*in pace*) was to say that in life they had realized what Christianity meant. It was the supreme compliment of the Christian community to a departed son or daughter.

For almost three hundred years after the death of Jesus, Christian writers were unanimously pacifistic when the topic of war and violence arose. Origen repeated the established teaching of early Christianity when he warned Christians lest "for warfare, or for the vindication of our rights, or for any occasion, we should take out the sword, for no such occasion is allowed by this evangelical teaching."[3] Hippolytus was a Roman churchman who drew up a list of the rules of discipline for Christians. Two of them concerned the question of military service. One said that a man could not be baptized as a Christian if he were in the army, and the other said that a candidate for Christianity who displayed military ambitions must be rejected because this "is far from the Lord."[4] Lactantius spoke the universal language of early Christianity when he said that killing is forbidden in such a way that "in this commandment of God, no exception at all ought to be made, that it is always wrong to kill a man whom God has wished to be regarded as a sacrosanct creature."[5] Lactantius also insisted that when God forbade killing, he didn't just forbid unjust killing by brigands, but also the kind of killing that is considered legal by most people.[6] Minucius Felix said that Christians had such a horror of bloodshed that they could not even bear to eat rare meat, lest they be offended by the sight of blood. Not only could Christians not kill, he said, but "it is not right for us either to see or hear a man being killed."[7]

In the third century, a non-Christian philosopher, Celsus, noting that all Christians were pacifists, worried about the future of the Roman empire if conversions to Christianity continued to increase. If everyone were like the Christians, he said, the empire "would be left in utter solitude and desertion and the forces of the empire would fall into the hands of the wildest and most lawless barbarians."[8] Origen, a Christian, undertook to answer Celsus's objection by saying that if all persons in the world became Christian you would need no army, because the spread of Christianity means the spread of peace. Also, he urged, if it was only all of Rome that became Christian, God would protect them, and so Celsus was not to worry.[9] Celsus's response to this is not recorded,

but the significant point is that Origen did not deny the charge
that Christians would not be soldiers. He conceded Celsus's point
that all Christians were pacifists. Strong church laws against sol-
diering and bloodshed continued in various parts of the Christian
church into the fifth century.

Early Christian pacifism was able to flourish under the protection of the *Pax* Romana. When that peace began to crumble,
Christians had to accommodate. Starting around the year 170,
Christians began to appear in the army, especially where the "barbarians" were attacking. But it was in the year 312, with the victory of Constantine at the Milvian Bridge, under the alleged auspices of Jesus, that Christians began their epochal turn to a new
morality of war and peace. As their social status changed suddenly
from persecution to preferment, a new world came into being. Im-
perial favor was a heady wine, and peaceful idealism staggered and
began to collapse. The befriending sword need not be beaten into
a plowshare. Christians crept out of the catacombs and were daz-
zled and beguiled by the state that had turned benevolent. Theology responded by interpreting the new events in terms of
blessedness, and the peace mission of the Christians waned. The
Christian Eusebius was beside himself with joy at the idea of a
Christian emperor. "The God of all, the supreme governor of the
whole universe by His own will appointed Constantine."[9a] (One
must recall some of the exultant endorsements of Ronald Reagan
by the new "Christian" right.) The Christian Lactantius rejoiced
that divine power could have appointed so superior a person "as
its agent and minister."[10] Constantine agreed. He said that he felt
called "to lead the nations to the service of the holiest law and to
spread the most blessed faith."[11] He avowed publicly to Jesus: "I
love your name and honor your power." And he promised to do
battle against Jesus' enemies.[12] He was as good as his word. As we
read in Eusebius: "He subdues and chastens the adversaries of the
truth according to the usages of war."[13]

Jesus had come full circle—from Prince of Peace to Lord of War.
Jesus, as war lord, was also active on the eastern front. A fourth-

century bishop of Nisibis reports that in response to prayer, the Lord routed the Persians by sending a cloud of mosquitoes and gnats to tickle the trunks of the enemy's elephants and the nostrils of his horses.[14] (Clearly, Jesus had not only waxed tough, but versatile.) The Christian abhorrence and avoidance of military service so changed that by the year 416 you had to be a Christian to serve in the Roman army.[15]

Theology, in the persons of such figures as Augustine and Ambrose, accommodated by baptizing the just-war theory of Plato and Cicero. The Augustinian accommodation, however, was not complete. Augustine, while allowing war under the aegis of the state, taught that it was wrong for a Christian to kill in his own self-defense.[16] He also harkened back to the earlier Christian pacifism, praising those Christians who died as martyrs rather than fight for their lives. Had they fought, he said, they would have been so numerous that nothing could have resisted them. Instead, they followed the example of Jesus who chose nonresistance and death.[17] Still, Augustine yielded, and allowed that wars could be fought, though, he insisted, this should be done in a mournful mood. He concluded reluctantly, and with an attitude more reminiscent of the library than of the battlefield: "Love does not exclude wars of mercy waged by the good."[18] As an enduring gesture to peace, the clergy who handled the sacraments of peace were forbidden to fight. And all the way to the eleventh century, soldiers who killed, even in a supposedly just war, had to perform rigorous penances. The accommodation to war was not without tension.

This tension, however, was all but lost in the barbarian invasion. These Christians were now gripped by a lust for battle. Their God was a God of war; their saints and heroes were warriors. The barbarians admired the empire that they overran, and also found the Christian faith of that empire attractive. They converted in droves. The waters of baptism, however, did not wash away their zest for battle. St. Michael, with his sword, replaced Wotan, their former god of war, as the patron of battle. In their liturgy they praised St. Peter, who used his sword to strike at the offending Roman. (They didn't bother to record Jesus' rebuke to Peter.) These newly converted Christians infused a mighty dose of violence into the already shaken cultural and moral atmosphere of the collapsing empire. Violence began to rage like a consuming libido.

The just-war theory became an irrelevant abstraction. Battles were fought on any pretext. It is recorded that a lord declared war on the city of Frankfurt because a lady of that city had refused to dance with his uncle. Elsewhere a cook, together with his scullions and dairymaids, issued a challenge of war to the Count of Salms. Even the clergy and the religious were gripped by the fever. The Archbishop of Mainz, on one occasion, sallied forth into battle and killed nine men with a club, rather than with a sword. With clerical nicety, he explained that he had chosen the club because the Christian faith abhors the shedding of blood. In a similarly hedged spirit, St. Gerald of Aurilliac went out to fight, but always with sword and spear turned backward so as to merely clobber the enemy without killing him. By a marvel of Providence, St. Gerald always won. In the midst of all this carnage, there appears St. Edmund, who went out and faced the Vikings alone and unarmed, and was slaughtered, standing for a Christ figure absorbing violence.[19]

In a vain effort to stem the violence, the Truce of God was instituted. Starting in the tenth century at the initiative of local bishops, the truce banned all fighting (under pain of excommunication) for several months around the feast of Easter, for the four weeks before Christmas, and on all Fridays, Sundays, and holy days. Church properties and the clergy were always to be exempt from violence, as were peasants and pilgrims, agricultural animals, and olive trees. From age twelve on, everyone was bound to take an oath to obey the truce and, with revealing irony, to take up arms against those who would not conform.[20] One of these oaths comes down to us from the tenth century, in a form taken by a gentleman who merited the name Robert the Pious. Its cagey wording tells much of the state of things. "I will not burn houses or destroy them, unless there is a knight inside. I will not root up vines. I will not attack noble ladies nor their maids nor widows or nuns, unless it is their fault. From the beginning of Lent to the end of Easter I will not attack an unarmed Knight."[21] Stanley Windass's remark comes to mind concerning the Truce of God: "The disease was too radical to respond to such first aid."[22]

What happened next was that the violence, which could not be contained, was, in effect, diverted into the Crusades. At the end of the eleventh century, the Crusades received formal blessing at the Council of Clermont. Their purpose: to reunite Christendom and establish Jerusalem as the center of Christian holiness. The sword had now been given first place in establishing the kingdom of God. The fury of these wars shows the danger of religious motivation for violence and recalls the dreadful dictum of John Calvin: "No heed is to be paid to humanity when the honor of God is at stake."[23] One report of the capturing of Jerusalem will convey the flavor of this sorry chapter in the medieval Christian consecration of violence.

> Some of our men (and this was more merciful) cut off the heads of their enemies; others tortured them longer by casting them into the flames. Piles of heads, hands and feet were to be seen in the streets of the city. . . . In the temple and portico of Solomon, men rode in blood up to their knees and the bridle reins. . . . This day, I say, marks the justification of all Christianity and the humiliation of paganism.[24]

A cargo of noses and thumbs sliced from the Saracens was sent back to the Greek emperor, in gory witness of the crusading zeal.[25]

Heresy, too, was fought with the sword as Christian warriors struck at the Cathari in southern France. Since there was a problem distinguishing the Cathari from the true believers, the instruction given was: "Kill them all; God will know which are his."[26]

Strains of the earlier pacifism reappeared eventually in various Christian groups—the Anabaptists, the Quakers, and the Franciscan Tertiaries. The Quakers represented the most effective reaction. They resisted the Augustinian tendency to leave to the state the decision on the justness of a war, and won from the English state exemption from conscription on conscientious grounds in 1802.

This, in capsule form, is what historical Christianity says on the issue of war and peace. It is, to say the least, a mixed bag. Clearly, the closer you get to the origins of Christianity, the more pacifistic and peace-centered it is. Of course, this was a luxury that could be indulged because of the Pax Romana which rested upon the military might of Rome. Accommodation did occur as that might diminished. The accommodation descended into a consecration of violence during the crusading period, as religious orders such as the Knights Templar were founded to go out and slay infidels in the name of Jesus Christ.

What is the bottom line on all of this? At the very least it seems that there is a strong concern for peace in the Christian message, and in the Hebrew scriptures on which Christianity was bred and nourished. *To be faithful in any way to the Christian tradition means having a bias for peace.* It means putting the burden of proof on the warrior, and not on the conscientious objector. The Crusader, with his bias for war, is a heretic to the Christian vision and to the Christian "God of Peace." Some Christians today opt to go back to the pacifism of the early Church. It would be rather "hard line" to argue that every Christian must take that stance. Those Christians could scarcely be considered beyond the pale who, while maintaining their commitment to peace, allow for the mournful possibility of some violence in self-defense, when all peaceful alternatives have been exhausted. But a lesser commitment than this to peace could not be, in any meaningful sense, of the word, Christian.

What then of the new Christian right? Clearly, they would not be at home in the early Church, where all war was considered incompatible with the vision of the Prince of Peace. Neither would they be comfortable with Augustine's theory of justifiable war. Augustine would still not permit killing in self-defense in a private setting. He would have opposed any gun lobby defending the right to bear arms. But the New Right is for a strong, well-armed defense at home and abroad, and are staunch defenders of the constitutional right of citizens to bear arms. They clearly are closest to the Crusaders. They do not have a horror of war; in fact they give it a sacred place in their assessment of God's plans. Theirs is the big-bang theory of the return of Jesus. War is, as we saw in Lindsey's popular book *The Late Great Planet Earth*, written into the scenario. It has a sacral role. This is the most frightening part of the New Right's religious faith.

In *The Fundamentalist Phenomenon*, coauthored by Jerry Falwell and two of his Liberty Baptist College professors, the following pompously phrased, but important statement is made: "No correct evaluation of Fundamentalism can properly be made without a proper assessment of the development and impact of dispensationalism upon the eschatology of the Evangelical Movement at the turn of the century."[27] Behind this language we can discern that what Falwell and his coauthors see as basic to fundamentalism is the following sort of biblical interpretation, which represents the philosophy of history that undergirds the New Right. It is called "dispensationalism" because it divides history into sections—dispensations—climaxing in the return and the millennial reign of Christ. Through an imaginative reading of Daniel 9 concerning the "seventy weeks," history is divided up nicely. The seventy weeks are made to be seventy "sevens" of years—totaling 490 years. Four hundred and eighty-three of these years refer literally to the period from the rebuilding of Jerusalem as recorded in Ezra and Nehemiah to the time of Jesus. After that, things do not follow in sequence. The coming of the final seven years is interrupted by the whole history of the Church. During this time-out, all kinds of things happen, many of them allegedly predicted in the Bible. Then the final seven years begins as a kind of countdown to the second coming of Christ, who will then reign for a thousand years. The final seven years is chock-full of presaged happenings. Indeed, so much is scheduled for that time that one wonders how God will get it all in. An anti-Christ will appear and be supported by apostate churches. The "Beast" of the book of Revelation will appear as a major political power. The Jews will return to Palestine, and some of them will be converted. The Jews will then go through a terrible "tribulation." But finally, as the seven years wind down, Jesus returns with a whole army of saints to defeat the hostile forces of the world powers—the Beast and the anti-Christ—in a place in the Near East known as Armageddon.[28]

Notice that in all of this human agency is not important. Dramatic divine interventions are the marking posts of history, particularly in this "latter-day" war to end all wars. As a result of the preannounced divine plan for war as a cleansing tool of holy Providence, this "dispensationalist" tradition has always been excited about wars that look like they could be the big one, and has likewise been wary of the prospects of a world without war. So, when the Hague Conference did not produce great promises of peace before World War I, fundamentalist writers were quick to point out that this was not surprising to those who knew the scriptures. Readers of the prophets know that true peace must await the return of the Prince of Peace. Before this second coming, any kind of peace that ensues will be of a counterfeit sort. It will be but the lull before the inevitable and necessary storm.[29] " 'Peace and safety' is what the world and apostate Christendom wants to hear. . . . The outbreak of sudden judgment will someday bring the terrible awakening."[30]

World War I was seen as potentially good news. For these people the calamities of war are promising harbingers of the blessed and triumphant return of the Lord. This same spirit had been apparent during the Civil War, which was greeted by millenialist Bible readers as "the glory of the coming of the Lord." Their excitement was exemplified by the Reverend William Gaylord, preaching to a church packed with blue-coated Union soldiers ready to depart for the front. He spoke of the day when the war would end.

> On! What a day that will be for our beloved land, when carried through a baptism of fire and blood, struggling through this birth-

night of terror and darkness, it shall experience a resurrection to a new life, and to a future whose coming glory already gilds the mountain tops. That day of future glory is hastening on. That day of a truer and deeper loyalty to God and to country—that day when the oppressor's rod shall be broken, when the sigh of no captive spirit shall be heard throughout all our fair land . . . the day of the Lord is at hand.[31]

As Professor James Moorhead writes in his study of this period: "What makes the 1860s especially interesting is the sheer intensity and virtual unanimity of Northern conviction that the Union armies were hastening the day of the Lord."[32] Moorhead notes how mischievous these bizarre interpretations were: "These grandiose expectations, incapable of realization in any event, contributed to a simplistic assessment of national problems and were among the many roots of America's unpreparedness to deal responsibly with Reconstruction or the legacy of slavery, let alone the other strange and bewildering difficulties on the far side of Appomattox."[33]

The noxious results of this mentality are considerable. The millenial fever, in any of its forms, leads to "a simplistic assessment of national problems," as Moorhead said, and wreaks severe problems at the level of national response. These visions give an alien interpretation of national destiny and policy. They impose a supernatural grid, into which national and international events are squeezed willy-nilly. They bring the seductive allure of simplism and divine drama to human affairs. This tendency is alive and well in the New Right.

We have seen it in Hal Lindsey. We see it in Tim LaHaye, who claims access to a detailed accounting of all the events regarding the coming destruction of Israel by Russia, etc.[34] The tribulation is coming, he warns us. LaHaye is also worried about false and counterfeit peace. Disarmament is a threat to him. He excoriates those who endorse homosexuality and the use of drugs, along with *"disarmament and everything else that is harmful to America."*[35] Obviously, disarmament is not helpful for advancing the day of the Lord—an event that essentially involves arms and slaughter—so it ends up in his list along with abuses such as drug addiction and that bugaboo of the right, homosexuality. Falwell has only scorn for the Strategic Arms Limitations Talks.[36] The "giveaway" of the Panama Canal treaty sticks painfully in his throat. The way we won it, the feelings of Latin America on the subject, and the relationship of all this to peace simply do not compute in his mind.[37] He bemoans the "no win" way in which we fought the war in Vietnam.[38] Clearly, there is no weapon in our arsenal that Falwell would have hesitated to use to assure victory. With stunning mental topsy-turvyness, he describes our current rate of arms production—which he sees as too slow—as a form of "unilateral disarmament."[39] The pace of increase of arms is not fast enough for Falwell. He even berates "peaceful intentions" as "acts of stupidity."[40]

As with the Crusaders, Falwell's God is a warrior god. He cites the participation of God in the 1967 "miraculous six-day war."[41] He describes it with great awe. There were the armies of Egypt, Jordan, Syria, and Lebanon poised and ready at the borders of Israel. Waiting behind them were the armies of Iraq, Algeria, Kuwait, and Sudan. War broke. Israel won, but deserves little credit for it. There was simply no way they could have won, General Falwell assures us, "had it not been for the intervention of God almighty."[42] Two points are again noteworthy here: the insignificance of human agency in human affairs, and enthusiasm for war as a sacramental medium. Humans are the pawns of God in His unfolding drama—which He was good enough to first predict in the Bible and then give the secret of interpretation to the pseudo-fundamentalists. The militaristic return of Jesus blesses war with a salvationist purpose. Again, the bias is *for* war, not against it. Here is the *Deus vult* (God wills it) of the Crusader, with millenial madness tossed in. Nothing remains of the bias for peace of the early Church.

Hal Lindsey carries this to the extent of a biblical prediction of final nuclear war. According to the apostle John, via Lindsey, every city in the world will be destroyed. One sees none of Augustine's mournful mood in the face of war when Lindsey excitedly predicts the final big bang. "Imagine, cities like London, Paris, Tokyo, New York, Los Angeles, Chicago—obliterated!" [43] According to Lindsey, the book of Revelation says that the eastern force, all by itself, will wipe out one-third of the world's population. Isaiah, in chapter 24, predicts that the Lord will "lay waste" the earth, scorch its inhabitants, with the result that only a few people will be left. Lindsey offers us one "bright spot" in all this gloom. Among the Jews who manage to survive this Armageddon, many will be converted to Jesus as their true Messiah. "The Greatest Moment," however, comes when the "great war" reaches such a pitch that it seems that no life will be left on earth. Then Jesus will return and save humankind from total self-extinction by preserving the faithful remnant. Again, in this tradition of manhandling the Bible, these events are not in any way peripheral. They are all part of what Lindsey calls "the main event." [44]

So important is "the main event" that one out of every twenty-five verses of the Christian part of the Bible is supposedly related to this second coming of Christ. So central is it to the Bible that there are five hundred predictions of it, whereas there were only three hundred predictions of the first coming of Christ. [45] When Jesus came the first time, he came as a lamb, willing to die to take away the sins of the world. Apparently Jesus has had enough of being portrayed as a lamb. Next time he will come "as a lion." [46] And what a lion! This is no longer the fourth-century Jesus, who settled for tickling the trunks of the enemy's elephants and the nostrils of his horses. His weapons are now earthquakes and thermonuclear blasts.

Jesus will make his return to earth on the Mount of Olives, from which he ascended into heaven. But as he touches down, the mountain will split in two with an enormous earthquake. A giant crevice will open in the earth, running from the Dead Sea to the Mediterranean. (An unidentified oil company, Lindsey tells us, found a fault line running exactly along that area that could activate at any time. It is awaiting, Lindsey tells us, "the foot." [47]) Those Jews who believe in Jesus will rush into the crevice—remembering Zechariah's prediction—and use it as a bomb shelter. And what will happen as they hide there in safety? There will be thermonuclear blasts. Zechariah gives us the details: "This shall be the plague wherewith the Lord will smite all the people that have fought against Jerusalem: their flesh shall consume away while they stand upon their feet, and their eyes shall consume away in their holes, and their tongue shall consume away in their mouth." (Zechariah 14:12) The biblical literalists have great imagination, but it does not take any imagination to compare this to a thermonuclear blast, which is what Lindsey does, and he adds: "It appears that this will be the case at the return of Christ." [48]

One wonders what will be left after this worldwide thermonuclear destruction. Not much, as far as the bodies of unbelievers go. Christian believers will have been lifted up in the great "rapture" to meet Christ "in the air." Jewish converts will have the crevice as a bomb shelter. As for the thermonuclear mess left everywhere, Christ will "put the atoms back together," and make a new heaven and a new earth where only *the good* will dwell.

The "good" will be a rather select group. It will not include any homosexuals, because homosexuality is a voluntary perversion, and there will be none of it in the "kingdom." There will be no Jews who prefer the religious richness of their own tradition for itself, and not as a prelude to conversion to pseudofundamentalist Christianity. There will be no liberals with giveaway programs that undermine the work ethic. There will be no noncapitalists. One would also not expect to see many Catholics, since they don't read the Bible the saved do. There will be few poor people and fewer blacks, since in the Falwellian gospel, God "prospers" the good. Since these people haven't been prospered, they couldn't have been good—so they won't be around.

The second coming as envisioned by these eccentrics will amount to a ruthless and a colossal right-wing purge. The hostility and truculence that is built into its conception is virtually without limit. With their simplistic *saved vs. unsaved* view of human life, they stand ready to write off most of humankind, commending them to death and hell. We have reached an extremity of hatred and militarism here. Early Christians would be baffled that such a terrifying scenario is presented in the name of Jesus of Nazareth, whom they found to be a person "meek and humble of heart."

In conclusion: because of their notion of history and of war as an instrument of salvation, the pseudofundamentalists have interests which are not in the national interest. Their incessantly avowed patriotism is secondary to their theological agenda. This is the core of their subversiveness. Their need for war comes from these two roots: they bear the legacy of militarized Christianity—they are Constantinian Christians and also Crusaders—and their dispensationalism and millenialism give war a providential value. Because they have not transcended the debits of Christian history, they import militarism, simplism and magic into the political process. Their power, therefore, deserves close watching.

Christians and Jews

Jerry Falwell believes that "God has blessed America because America has blessed the Jew."[49] But remember that he also says that Jews are spiritually blind and desperately in need of Jesus.[50] He further says that the hope of reversing the moral decay of America lies with the "Christian" people of America.[51] All of which comes to a rather dubious "blessing" for the allegedly spiritually blind, Messiah-killing, Messiah-denying, moral-decay-promoting Jews. There are no people among us more meriting of suspicion than Christians patting themselves on their backs for their benevolence to Jews. The purpose of historical consciousness is to discover what spirits lurk in our intentions. No Christian with even a smattering of historical knowledge can be confident that only the milk of human kindness toward Jews flows in Christian veins. I am not saying, "Show me your history and I will tell you what you are." But I am saying, "Show me your history, and then prove to me that you have transcended its negativities." If historical consciousness means nothing—as is true for the New Right—then the suspicion grows that the shadows of historical negativities could be heavy. A brief, illustrative look at the history of the Christian treatment of Jews is good for the Christian soul. It is not a flattering picture.

Some years ago a Catholic priest, Edward Flannery, was walking on Park Avenue in New York City in the company of a young Jewish couple. They passed a large illuminated cross that was part of a Christmas display. The young woman looked at the cross and trembled visibly. "That cross makes me shudder," she said. "It is like an evil presence."[52] The pursuit of the causes of that shudder led Flannery to the writing of his book *The Anguish of the Jews*.

Anti-Semitism has wracked the Christian soul from the beginning. The break of the Christian Church from the Synagogue was a bitter one. Starting with the gospels, the Jews are cast in a grievously guilty light. They are pictured as screaming for the crucifixion of Jesus and are made to say, "His blood be upon us and our children!" (Matthew 27:26) This symbol of guilt pervaded centuries of Christian and Jewish relations. As to the question of whether Christian anti-Semitism goes back to our origins, one Christian theologian, F. Lovsky, states the case bluntly: "In the final analysis there can be no debate. There are too many signs that stake out the permanence, the importance and the gravity of Christian anti-Semitism: contempt, calumnies, animosity, segregation, forced baptisms, appropriation of children, unjust trials, pogroms, exiles, systematic persecutions, thefts and rapine, hatred, open or concealed, social degradation."[53]

Even that listing of horrors is incomplete. A look at church law is revealing, because laws express and rely upon broad consent and approval. Laws are windows into a culture. The laws of the Christian churches have enough anti-Semitism in them to make anyone shudder. Intermarriage and sexual intercourse between Christians and Jews were forbidden at the Synod of Elvira in 306. The same synod forbade Christians and Jews to eat together. The synod of Clermont, in 535, banned Jews from holding public office. Jews were forbidden by the Synod of Orlean, in 538, to employ Christian servants or to possess Christian slaves. The same synod banned them from the streets during Eastertime. The Talmud and other Jewish books were publicly burned at the Synod of Toledo in 681, which, of course, taught the faithful a starkly symbolic lesson about the hideous contents of these books. Christians could not patronize Jewish doctors (Trulanic Synod, 692). They could not live in Jewish homes (Synod of Narbonne, 1050). Jews could not be plaintiffs or witnesses against Christians in court (Third Lateran Council, 1179). The same council said Jews were not permitted to withhold inheritance from children who converted to Christianity. The Fourth Lateran Council cancelled all debts that Crusaders owed to Jews. This council also reinstituted the old Christian custom of confining Jews to a ghetto and making them wear distinctive badges, which took on various forms. In France, the Jews had to wear a yellow sphere, the *rouelle*. In Germany, they wore a special hat; in Poland, a pointed hat. In Sicily, the wearing of a circular badge was mandated. The Council of Oxford, in 1222, prohibited the construction of new synagogues. Christians could not rent or sell real estate to Jews (Synod of Ofen, 1279). The Council of Basel prohibited Jews from acting as agents in contracts involving Christians, and also banned them from obtaining academic degrees.

Clearly, the Nazis had a lot to build on when they banned intermarriage, barred Jews from dining cars, limited their employment possibilities, restricted them to ghettos, kept them off the streets on Nazi holidays, imposed special taxes, limited their rights in courts, voided their wills, made them mark their clothes, homes, and stores, limited their access to universities and other schools, and seized their real estate. There is a long and terrible sequence in all this. Raul Hilberg wrote: "[the Nazis] did not discard the past; they built upon it. They did not begin a development; they completed it."[54] And as A. Roy Eckardt says, the facts of the case make "ludicrous any unqualified claim that the Nazis were the enemies of Christendom. In actuality, they were in very large measure the agents for the 'practical' application of an established social logic."[55]

Even the actual genocidal attempt of Hitler had Christian precedent. When the first Crusade began in 1066, it turned first on
the Jews. As one chronicler of the period puts it, the Crusaders of
Rouen said: "We desire to combat the enemies of God in the east;
but we have under our eyes the Jews, a race more inimical to God
than all the others. We are doing this whole thing backwards."[56]
They immediately corrected themselves and fell upon the Jews,
slaughtering as much as a quarter or a third of the Jewish population in Germany and northern France at that time.[57] In Rameru
in France, the famous Jewish scholar Jacob Tam "had five wounds
inflicted upon his head in vengeance for the five wounds of
Christ."[58] This earlier holocaust was repeated throughout later history. Starting in 1298, an army of Judenschächter (Jewslaughter-
ers) moved through Germany and Austria on a mission of murder.
They are reported to have decimated one-hundred-and-forty communities of Jews, killing as many as one hundred thousand persons.

That is but a bit of evidence of the poison we Christians carry in
the historical marrow of our bones. As a Catholic, I grew up pray-
ing on Good Friday for the "perfidious Jews" (*pro perfidis Judaeis*).
Only with recent Catholic reforms was that obscenity erased from
Catholic prayer. Could I, or any Christian bred of such a tradition,
stand and proclaim that we are blessed by God because we have
blessed the Jews? The claim should choke us a little. It does not
bother Jerry Falwell or the other New Rightists, who feel that their
strategic interest in Israel gives them a plenary indulgence and full
pardon for anti-Semitic sins.

As a sign of the continuity of Christian anti-Semitism into the
present, Bethany Press, in 1973, published a book entitled *The
Bible, the Supernatural and the Jews*, by McCandish Phillips. The
cover shows the flames of hell arising from infernal regions and
encompassing a broken tablet marked with Hebrew lettering. The
author argues that the Jews, being chosen, were more powerfully
evil than mere gentiles when they fell away from God. The author
goes on to implicate Jews, with their superior talent for evil, in

such things as satanism, drugs, rock music, and the overall break-
down of traditional morality.

Civilization depends on the possibility of transcending the sins
of the past. It is naive, however, to assume that perfect transcendence will be the result of our best efforts. For the New Right,
however, no effort at transcendence is visible. Those who proclaim
themselves moral develop no skills in the art of conscience-prob-
ing.

Both history and their eccentric biblical interpretation combine
to make the New Right anti-Semitic. The candor of the Reverend
Bailey Smith when he said that God does not hear the prayers of
Jews—and the momentary candor of Jerry Falwell when he immediately agreed—tells the tale. In pointing out the theological
depths of the anti-Semitism of the New Right, Smith and Falwell
were saying that even God is anti-Semitic. There is no way to the
Father-God, except through Jesus, for the Smiths and the Falwells. No politic disclaimer from Falwell can counter the solid position of New Right religionists, that those who are not Christians
are failures religiously and morally. No one could hold that view
and then grant the beauty of or the authenticity of Jewish religious
experience or tradition. No one could hold the pseudofundamentalist beliefs that permeate the New Right and not be at least a
partial heir of the anti-Semitism that disgraces Christian history. A
few Jews are heartened by the pro-Israel stance of the New Right.
Most are more perceptive. They look at the New Right and shudder. They know the old story too well.

New Right Racism

New Right preachers are hell and brimstone preachers. They
take pride in calling evil by its name and in dangling sordid sins
before us. Their writings overflow with lists of sins and human
atrocities. *On none of those lists do we find racism.* That fact alone
is indicting.

The racism of the New Right shows up in two forms: first, they insult black persons with the "blame the victim" strategem, or by simply rendering them invisible. Secondly, they attack solutions to black problems and the agencies and programs that promote these solutions. In all of this, the New Right shows themselves to be the children of the historical racism that afflicted large portions of the Christian churches in this country.

There is greatness in American Christian history regarding justice for black people. The attack on slavery owes much to solid evangelical Protestant piety. The civil rights efforts after the Civil War and after World War II were fueled by, among other things, a biblically grounded sense of justice. However, self-congratulation would be myopic. Historically, the record is not all edifying. Protestant historian Martin Marty says in his study of the Protestant experience in America: "The Protestant empire was built at the expense of black inhabitants. They were either to be overlooked, intentionally neglected, enslaved, expatriated, or exterminated. . . . The community of reconciliation taught America how to divide, for it was an early agent of segregation in all its forms."[59] Christians owe it to honesty to inquire in their consciences whether it is that legacy that is reflected in their choices, or the gentle, humanizing values of the gospel. The black preacher Richard Allen wrote these words before his death in 1831: "This land, which we have watered with our tears and our blood, is now our mother country."[60] In one part of the American-Christian story—including the Protestant and Roman Catholic sectors—that hard-won nationalization has been persistently denied. The black person did not fit in an America that must be "Christian" as well as white. The Indians learned this quickly. So did the blacks, who were brought here but were never fully allotted human or citizen status. Dr. Hugh Williamson, in 1811, gave the purest statement of this "white American" dream. Over a long period of time, he wistfully surmised, God would alter blacks so that they would become white. That was Williamson's *ultimate solution* to the racial problem. It also symbolizes how deep the racial hatred ran.

The techniques of insult against blacks employed by the New

Right are varied. In the invisibility approach, blacks seem not to exist. Thanks to free enterprise, exults Falwell, America has enjoyed the highest standard of living in the world.[61] In reality, that is true only for parts of white America. Black people have lived in permanent recession or depression in this country. "The system is excellent," Senator Jesse Helms assures us.[62] It is not excellent for those blacks within it who are at least twice as likely to be unemployed as whites, and who are confined to ghettos where there are often more rats than people. Talk of prosperity that ignores black poverty implies that irrelevance of blacks. That is racism.

The insult also takes the form of implying that employment and wealth come to the good. Falwell believes that there are now enough jobs to go around.[63] If so, what does that do to the image of the unemployed? Obviously, they don't want the jobs. As the myth goes—and the New Right misses no opportunity to spread it—the poor do not want to work. "Will they live off giveaway programs . . . forever?" bewails Falwell.[64] This implies "they" have a choice. It ignores studies that have shown that the poor really do want to work, that they value the meaning that comes from work as much as do those who are well off.[65] A thorough study done at the Brookings Institute concluded (in contradiction to the prevailing myth): "This study reveals no difference between poor and nonpoor when it comes to life goals and wanting to work."[66] This study has been confirmed by others in California, New York, and Louisiana. The view of the New Right, however, is that the poor do not want to work. Since blacks are worst off in employment statistics, the implication is clear. They are lazy and immoral. Their poverty is not our problem; it is theirs. Therefore, do not trouble us with affirmative action. Let the white cream rise to the top without interference.

Blacks clearly need public schools. The New Right is mercilessly critical of public schools, and claims to be opening three new "Christian" schools a day as an alternative to them. Even the very concept of "racial rights" is abhorrent to the New Right. LaHaye sees three decades of evil unfolding in this way: the 1960s brought the battle for racial rights, the 1970s for sexual rights, and the

1980s aim to destroy religious rights.[67] The sequence here is a sequence of evils, commencing with the efforts to give human and civil rights to the blacks and ending with the destruction of religious rights. What humanists call "rights," real Christians call "wrongs," he tells us.[68] Groups supporting blacks are labeled evil and atheistic. These include the NAACP, the Urban League, and the Dubois Clubs.

The New Right is all too clearly linked to indentured racism on the American scene. They embody an historical legacy without any apparent awareness of the historical perversions that influence their racial attitudes. Is it surprising that they have great sympathies for the white Christians of South Africa? The only problem they see in that part of the world, where apartheid strips blacks of minimal human rights and dignity, is the threat of communism.[69] This mentality of the past, which they continue to manifest on racial matters, would not fit them to perceive the evil of apartheid.

The New Right is a force aimed at shutting down the second civil rights movement in this country. If the first civil rights movement, which began with the Civil War, definitely ended with *Plessy vs. Ferguson* in 1896, the second, which symbolically began with the Brown decision in 1954, may have ended with the elections of November 4, 1980. The New Right wielded important influence in that election. The president whom they supported has been taking all the steam out of civil rights programs. By neglect, slowdown, and the appointment of "sensible" people to key positions in civil rights agencies, the means and the spirit needed to maintain progress on that front are being crippled. This scandalous collapse of morality is supported by the self-proclaimed "Christian" and "pro-moral" New Right. Hypocrisy could scarcely be made of more sordid stuff.

Anti-Catholicism

Anti-Catholicism has been called "the pornography of the Puritan."[70] The deviant fundamentalist strain has always been strongly anti-Catholic. These were the people who put the Catholicism of

Al Smith and, more recently, John Kennedy on trial. Historically, it was not just the right wing that was so phobic of Catholicism. Martin Marty writes: "Conservatives like Samuel F.B. Morse, moderates like Lyman Beecher, and liberals like Horace Bushnell joined in the massive Protestant attempt to make a bogey out of the miniscule Catholic presence. The evangelicals were constantly hearing rumors that the Pope was to concentrate Roman energies on winning the West, having failed so miserably in the original thirteen colonies."[71] In large parts of the evangelical movement, the pope was associated with the evils to be overcome in "the latter days." In 1798, the pope's exile from Rome was seen as the expulsion of "the Beast," which was to come prior to the return of Jesus.

The overall Protestant hegemony that developed in America was not notably friendly to Catholic interests. Protestantism enjoyed unofficial establishment status in a way that Catholics have never known. As J.M. O'Neill writes: "Practically every public school system in America used public money and property for the promotion of Protestantism until the period of the Civil War, and many of them long after that time."[72] At times, Protestant pressure became muscular: "Catholic children were flogged in a number of states for refusing to take part in the compulsory Protestant religious services in the public schools. In Philadelphia in 1842 when the Catholic Bishop Kenrick respectfully asked that the Catholic children be allowed to use their own version of the Bible, and that they be excused from other religious instruction in the public school, there ensued two years of bitterness and mob violence, the burning of two Catholic churches and a seminary, and finally three days of rioting in which thirteen people were killed and fifty wounded—in the City of Brotherly Love."[73]

However, one might argue that at least in this regard, the New Right has sloughed off the historical weight of prejudice and joined forces with Catholics. It is true that, for one thing, the horrors of communism has united conservative Catholics and Protestants in the past quarter-century. Communism seemed more of a threat than the papal forces, and it was natural for the paranoid right to switch to the more plausible enemy—making allies with their former Roman enemies in the process. Also, commonly felt issues constitute a bonding force. The traditional antiabortion stance of Catholics is much admired on the New Right. Some ultraconservative Catholics, in turn, are drawn to the New Right as their church undergoes the unsettling process of overdue reform. Catholicism has its own fundamentalism. About 15 percent of Pat Robertson's 700 Club audience is Catholic. It is estimated that Catholics contributed twice as much money last year to The 700 Club as they did to the bishops' communications collection.[74] Catholicism is no longer the political hazard it was with ultraright voters. Alabama elected Jeremiah Denton as its first Republican senator in one hundred years and the first Catholic ever. Paul Weyrich, himself an Eastern Rite Catholic, is a veteran lobbyist and organizer for the New Right. He is confident that Catholics are natural candidates for New Right politics. "Catholics in this country do not differ with the views of Moral Majority on most issues," says Weyrich.[75] Pope John Paul II, because of his many conservative utterances on issues of sexuality, is looked on as a member of the New Right. Jerry Falwell calls him "the best hope we Baptists ever had."[76] Weyrich thinks American bishops are a problem, since he sees them as part of the "old liberal elite." However, "Pope John Paul is on our side and the people are on our side, so the American bishops will increasingly discover that the vise is tightening both from the top and the bottom"[77]

In spite of all this, it would be well to remember that the arc of conversion from prejudice is a wide one. Sharp turns are not anticipated. Catholics would be well advised to realize that they do not have a "lasting city" in the New Right. In January 1981, Dr. Curtis Hitson, who is the editor of the *Sword of the Lord*, a suggestively entitled, widely circulated fundamentalist paper, refused to appear at a James Robison Bible Conference because Phyllis Schlafly was appearing there, and "she is a Roman Catholic." Hitson reminded his fellow fundamentalists that Catholicism has been "a growing accumulation of error through the years, with new doctrines being added continually."[78]

In the book *The Fundamentalist Phenomenon*, which attempts to be a mediating and moderating influence, anti-Catholicism still slips through. We read about the "return-to-Rome emphasis within the Anglican Church" which "ultimately resulted in the *defection* of John Henry Newman to Catholicism."[79] In that same volume we read that the outstanding characteristic of fundamentalism in the last thirty years is its firm commitment to "separatism."[80] This means a determined withdrawal from all evangelical and Christian groups who are tainted with "liberalism" of any sort. This passion for "separatism" was seen in the fundamentalist rejection of Billy Graham. A number of incidents led to Graham's downfall. They are spelled out for us in *The Fundamentalist Phenomenon*. Among his sins we find that he preached at a Roman Catholic institution, Belmont Abbey College, in 1965, and accepted an honorary degree from that same institution in 1968. Also, in a 1969 Congress on Evangelism sponsored by Graham, morning devotions were conducted by a Roman Catholic priest. In 1971, a Catholic priest cooperated in the Graham Crusade in Oakland, California. In 1973, Graham preached at a Catholic cathedral and participated in a funeral mass. In the listing of Graham's indiscretions, five out of ten refer to some collusion with Catholics.[81]

Tim LaHaye also reminds us that St. Thomas Aquinas undermined Christian culture and education by trusting in human reason too much and bringing in the teachings of non-Christian philosophers. Western man's defection to secular humanism was midwifed by Thomas Aquinas.[82] Since this nebulous concept called "secular humanism" is the very bane of all that is good and godly, Catholics cannot be forgiven their support of it.

The New Right thinks and acts out of a past they do not know and, therefore, cannot criticize. The uncriticized past has the power to hold with a demonic grip. Political discourse that is not historically grounded is fatally flawed. The positions of the New Right toward women, war and peace, non-Anglo Saxons, education, Jews, the role of government, social justice, and a number of other issues are under the unchallenged control of the past. The New Right uses the Bible to bypass history. All their claims are "Bible-based," as though history never happened. This use of the Bible as a substitute for historical consciousness is a cardinal defect in New Right thinking. If deviant Christian fundamentalism is to be with us and active in our politics—and history does not support the view that they will quickly depart—we must attend to their amnesia.

Chapter Five

BLUEPRINT FOR
A FASCIST FAMILY

The term "family" is a catchall word for the New Right. It involves much more than warm feelings for that social unit commonly consisting of mom, dad, and the kids. Using "family" as the model for the state, and "family" issues as models for New Right legislative action, the so-called *family question* covers a broad terrain. It supplies New Right tactics for majority tyranny. It includes the New Right platform for male and heterosexual dominance in society. It covers the issue of public control of private morality in the abortion dispute. And it encompasses the New Right's plans for the education of our children. All of these issues appear in the Family Protection Act, which is a bible of New Right thought, and in the various "human life" amendments. Through these and other efforts, the New Right seeks to control our families, our schools, and our political freedoms. The spirit of the assault is seen in this statement by Falwell: "The problem is that we don't agree with those buzzards—and that we outnumber them!"[1] Let the "buzzards," therefore, beware!

For one thing, the Family Protection Act (S 1808) would deny federal funds to schools using texts that "would tend to denigrate, diminish or deny the role differences between the sexes *as it has been historically understood in the United States.*"[2] When you consider what the historical attitude toward women has been in the United States, that becomes an alarming project. An editorial in the *New York Herald* of September 12, 1882 catches the flavor of how women were seen in our history.

> How did woman first become subject to man, as she now is all over the world? By her nature, her sex, just as the negro is and always will be to the end of time, inferior to the white race and, therefore, doomed to subjection; but she is happier than she would be in any other condition, just because it is the law of her nature.[3]

The Family Protection Act would like to make this "law of her nature" the law of the land. This legislative effort, which does us the favor of summing up much of the agenda of the New Right, is a fearsome thing. What we hear throughout its pages are the voices of Falwell, LaHaye, and William Jennings Bryan. The hand, however, is that of Senator Paul Laxalt, trying to give New Right visions the standing of law.

The Family Protection Act opens with the acknowledgment that "a stable and healthy American family is at the foundation of a strong American society." Senator Laxalt, in introducing the act, said that the family "is the basis of our very existence as a nation; it is the bedrock upon which our whole Nation as well as our society is based."[4] Herein lies the clue for understanding this document and the other legislative efforts of the New Right. These men see a strong link between family and society. The family for them is the workshop for the state. The picture they paint of family life is what their state would look like. The state is the family writ large. However, the family they project for us is fascist, sexist, and racist. So too is their state. The core of fascism is the fear of freedom. The Family Protection Act would inhibit the freedom of all those who disagree with them. It would encourage private Falwellian-type schools, remove from them the supervision of the National Labor Relations Board, and keep the Internal Revenue Service off their backs. (The IRS, of course, is concerned about segregation in "Christian" schools.) It would take legal services away from those who disagree with the New Right on issues of "divorce, abortion, gay rights, and school desegregation."[5]

Laxalt admits that in his view the family is a religious matter, indeed "one of the fundamental cornerstones of our entire Judaeo-Christian tradition." Ideally, he says, family matters can be left to religious leaders. "But the family is now facing social and political threats of such magnitude as to compel a political defense."[6] This amounts to a political defense for a religious position on what the "bedrock" family and educational system of our nation should be. The school system is an extension of the family, and must be under "Christian" control. In this view, the Family Protection Act would strangle the public schools, which have strayed from New Right dogma, and encourage the spread of "Christian" schools, which, as Tim LaHaye tells us, are sprouting at the rate of one every seven hours, and which by 1992 will, he hopes, be teaching 51 percent of American school children.[7]

The act would also inhibit the protection of abused children and battered wives, while giving legal standing to spanking and school prayer. As Rosemary Ruether sums up the message of the act, "its assumption is that if only women and children were reduced to their traditional dependency in the patriarchal family, made to pray regularly and shielded from disturbing new ideas, all would be well and America would again become 'strong.' "[8] This is the blueprint for family and national life that the United States Senate is being asked to dignify with the status of law.

Prohibition II

In tandem with the Family Protection Act are the various efforts to introduce abortion prohibition. This would appear to be a narrow moral crusade but it is broad in its thrust. These prohibitionists, whose ideological parents told us that we could not have a drink in this country because it bothered their consciences, now want to tell women they cannot exercise their consciences on the widely debated issue of abortion. The antiabortion movement is not just a private cause of those "prolife" persons whose respect for life seems fixated on the prenatal period. Rather, we have here the start-off point of attack of a whole range of civil liberties and human rights. The nature and intent of the antiabortion movement illustrate the whole approach of the New Right to the political order. It does, of course, represent, another major effort by the disseminators to tell the childbearers what they may or may not do, but beyond that it is an effort to impose one of *many* possible moral views on the entire polity. But what is the reality?

All Fertilized Eggs are Created Equal

In 1973, the United States Supreme Court ruled that in view of the emotional, physical, and mental pressures involved in childbearing, the right to privacy was broad enough to include a woman's decision to terminate or not to terminate a pregnancy. The Court refused to say when personal life begins, noting that there was no consensus on this point among religious and philosophical sources. The Court felt that this determination is a religious and medical problem and not one the judiciary could make. The debate dates back to antiquity, so the Court was properly modest in suggesting that it could not end this debate by decree.[9]

The abortion prohibitionists are now out to end that debate by legislation, thus rendering moot the decisions of the Supreme Court. Various versions of a Human Life Amendment are circulating. The majority of the National Right to Life Committee approve the following one:

Section 1. The right to life is the paramount and most fundamental right of a person.

Section 2. With respect to the right to life guaranteed to persons by the fifth and fourteenth articles of amendment to the Constitution, the word "person" applies to all human beings, irrespective of age, health, function, or condition of dependency, including their unborn offspring at every stage of biological development including fertilization.

Section 3. No unborn person shall be deprived of life by any person; Provided, however, that nothing in this article shall

prohibit a law permitting only those medical procedures
required to prevent the death of a pregnant woman; but
this law must require every reasonable effort be made to
preserve the life and health of the unborn child.

Section 4. Congress and the several States shall have power to enforce this article by appropriate legislation.

The crux of the matter is in Section 2 which expresses the extremist view that personhood exists from the moment of fertilization. The Supreme Court recognized that not even conservative
churches are in agreement on that point. For example, a Roman
Catholic scholar and priest, Joseph Donceel, S.J., voices a long-
tenured Catholic view when he writes: "There can be no mind
before the organism is ready to carry one, and no spirit before the
mind is capable of receiving it. . . . I feel certain that there is no
human soul, hence no human person, during the first few weeks
of pregnancy, as long as the embryo remains in the vegetative stage
of its development."[10] Charles E. Curran, a priest and theologian
at the Catholic University of America, states a common opinion
among Catholic theologians when he says: "In conflict situations I
would allow abortion to save human life or for other values that
are commensurate with human life. This would obviously include
grave but real threats to the psychological health of the woman and
could also include other values of a socio-economic nature in extreme situations."[11] Protestant theologian James Nelson sums up
the Protestant position on abortion: "The perspectives range along
a continuum from anti-abortion to abortion-on-request, with perhaps the large number of ethicists and Protestant groups affirming
the justifiable but tragic abortion in certain situations of value conflict."[12]

Jewish theology is also divided on the abortion issue. The *Encyclopedia of Bioethics* reports: "Differences continue to exist within
Judaism. The only authoritative text on therapeutic abortion in the
Talmud recognizes that the fetus becomes truly human only if the
greater part of it is already born. . . . All authors in the orthodox
and conservative cultural traditions accept the therapeutic abortion

necessary for the life of the mother and, according to some, also for the mental health of the mother. . . . Within the reformed branch of Judaism there is a greater willingness to attribute less value to the fetus. It is indistinguishable from the mother and may be destroyed for the mother's sake, just as a person may decide to sacrifice a bodily limb to cure a worse malady."[13]

As far as the Bible is concerned, the Christian Scriptures (New Testament) say nothing at all about abortion. The first five books of the Hebrew Scriptures (Old Testament), which contain the fundamental law (Torah) of the Jews, only takes up the problem of accidental abortion. Exodus 21:22–25 considers the case when two men are fighting and one happens to strike a pregnant woman, causing an abortion. If there is no injury to the woman, the man only has to pay a fine. If there is injury to the woman, the "law of the talion" was invoked, requiring "an eye for an eye," "a life for a life," etc. As Reverend John Connery, S.J., writes: "This has generally been interpreted to mean that the fetus was not considered a human being. If it were, the *lex talionis* would apply and the penalty would be 'a life for a life,' which would be the penalty if the mother herself died."[14]

Science, too, has discomfiting news for the abortion prohibitionists. First, for the first week after fertilization, while the cell mass is as yet undifferentiated, two things are biologically possible: twinning and recombination. In other words, the cell mass may split (or be split) into two, and when the cells begin to differentiate, two fetuses will develop. Also, where there are two cell masses developing, the two may conjoin into one, resulting eventually in only one baby.[15] In our experience, "persons" do not have the power to split into two individuals. Neither can two "persons" become one by biological conjuncture. Whatever these premature cell masses are, they are not persons in an intelligible sense of that term.

Yet another embarrassment awaits the prohibitionists. Scientists estimate that 70 percent of all fertilized ova never survive the natural processes to birth. 58 percent never even manage to implant.[16] Given the idiosyncrasies of the deviant fundamentalists, this raises frightening specters. If God is in charge of nature, and if God wastes 70 percent of all fertilized ova—"persons" in the Human Life Amendment view—God is guilty of the mass slaughter of American citizens. Might some deviant fundamentalists not be tempted to go one step further than the Scopes trial and conduct a trial of God for his homicidal negligence in failing to guide most conceived "persons" to their birth? Indeed, in line with the mentality of the Human Life Amendment people, God becomes the Master Abortionist.

The traditional American approach to moral debates vis-à-vis the law is fundamentally sound. Where there is solid consensus, there can be a law reflecting that consensus. All agree that stealing is bad, and so we have laws against it. We all agree that the unprovoked killing, with "malice aforethought" of born persons is wrong, and so we have outlawed it. We all agree that a degree of literacy is necessary to function in modern life, and so we require some education. However, the abortion issue does not fit into the category of *law expressing consensus*. The spectrum of opinions in this debate is broad. Let me illustrate the extremities within which the abortion debate rages. At the permissive extreme, I would place Professor Mary Anne Warren, a philosopher at San Francisco State University. Dr. Warren was asked to comment on a case involving a man in desperate need of a kidney, with no prospective donor in sight who has the type needed for the transplant. The moral question concerned the plan of the man and his wife to seek pregnancy, in order to abort and use the fetus's kidneys for transplant. Warren approved this plan of action. She found "no serious moral objection to killing a fetus, an entity far below the threshold of personhood, in order to save the life of an adult human being."[17] Warren's position is that "a proper respect for the right to life requires that it not be respected where it does not exist."[18] I suggest that this is about as permissive a position as one could offer. If one may morally use a fetus as an organ farm because it lacks a right to life, then it follows one may end its life for almost any reason; that is an extreme position. However, the Human Life Amendment position that a fertilized egg is a person and a citizen of the United States is also an extreme one—at the opposite end of the spectrum.

A number of other positions lie between these two extremes. There are a variety of situations in which the question of abortion arises, and one may be open to some abortions and not others. Some situations in which abortions are defended are these: to save the life of the mother; to preserve the mental health of the mother, especially in cases of rape, incest, youthfulness, poverty, and profound mental retardation of the mother; when amniocentesis reveals a serious genetic disease in the fetus; to complete an incipient miscarriage; upon discovery of serious communicable disease in the mother; or simply as a backup for contraceptive failure. Some people approve all of these reasons for abortions, some approve of none, and some approve of a few of them. There may be some consensus on the right to abortion to save the life of the mother, but beyond this, disagreement prevails. What we have here is not a consensus such as would support a law. The Prohibition experience, in which all alcoholic beverages were banned by constitutional amendment, shows the hazard of forcing a law upon a society without a sufficient base of consent. It failed, and bred other evils.

The abortion debate is an example of what I would call respectable debate. What is a respectable debate? As I have written elsewhere: "A moral option comes within respectable debate if it is supported by serious reasons which commend themselves to many people, and if it has been endorsed by a number of authorities in the field of ethics, and if has been approved by reputable religious or other humanitarian bodies."[19] In a situation of respectable debate a number of opinions are held and disputed within a society that have some significant force and persuasiveness, and which commend themselves to persons and institutions that are not known for utter eccentricity. If some group wanted to defend human sacrifice, they could not claim immunity under the rubric of "respectable debate." The criteria mentioned above would not be met. In the complex abortion debate, however, those criteria are met. Humane persons, whether religious or not, take differing positions on this subject. Their positions find support in the major religious bodies and in the various humanitarian institutions and professions. Moral quandaries do not always allow for certitude. Doubt, at times, survives our most intense investigations. A humane society will try not to excommunicate any competing moral views that commend themselves to good persons in doubtful and debated matters.

In the American tradition, this is particularly true if the debate is partially religious in character. The American instinct here has been to allow the greatest possible freedom. Part of the motivation behind rejecting the tradition of an "established" religion was to prevent one religious view from becoming official, to the detriment of free and respectful debate. The instinct of the abortion prohibitionists is fascistic and elitist. The fascist decides what is truth and what is error, and then decrees that error has no rights. That is not the American way.

There is another defect in this effort to legislate a sectarian religious view on abortion. As things stand now in the United States, no one is required by law to have an abortion. The devotees of the Human Life Amendment are free to avoid abortion and to persuade others to do likewise. That, however, is not enough for them. They insist on disenfranchising those who disagree with them, for in their arrogant view, disagreement with them on heartfelt issues is never respectable. Some people may argue that the Supreme Court's decisions on abortion are too permissive. But even if that case can be made, the fact remains that no abortions are compulsory in this country. *Legislation or rulings that inhibit freedom bear the burden of proof more than laws or rulings that extend freedom.* The best minds of the major religious and ethical traditions have long contended on this issue. Now the New Right would simply legislate an end to this ancient debate. This would be a use of the democratic process that contradicts the nature of a free society.

The burden of proof here cannot be met. It also brings the state into decision making about reproduction in a most intimate way. The precedent for this is Nazi, not American. .

It is not easy to believe that the New Right's opposition to abortion comes from a delicate sensitivity to human life in fetal form. The New Right wants to rob social services and increase preparations for war, and war is fatal to fetuses as well as to born persons. Their position must be seen in terms of their whole agenda. Their primary concern is power. Their literature bewails weak fathers who do not practice stern discipline over their wives and children. They are strong on censorship, hating as they do any ideas other than their own. They want a strong United States with first-strike potential to destroy all potential enemies. Their interest in abortion—we may fairly suspect—relates also to power and control. If a woman has control over her own body and her pregnancy, she has considerable power. This threatens the patriarchs. Also, there is political power to be gained in the abortion issue. It brings in other right-wing groups. Under the "family-issue" rubric, New Right activists, like Weyrich and Phillips, have labored to bring together single-issue groups with different interests. As Frances Fitzgerald observes: "They managed to create the ecumenical atmosphere in which Falwell and other fundamentalists, who had initially paid no attention to *Roe v. Wade,* put abortion at the head of their list of abominations."[20] Again, the alleged pro-family concern is part of a larger political agenda. The antiabortion fervor is related to the New Right's desire to unite single-issue groups under their leadership.

The New Rightists say they want to save the family and remove government from people's private lives so they can do good and avoid evil and educate their children in the good old American way. In fact, both the Family Protection Act and the Human Life Amendment would put the government into family life in an entirely new way. The Family Protection Act would deny federal funds to any project that offends ultraconservative standards; effectively, this puts the government heavily on the backs of teachers and school boards. So much for educational freedom in a pluralistic society! The Human Life Amendment, by giving citizen status to fertilized eggs, legitimizes government's compelling interest in what goes on in the privacy of the womb. If the intrauterine contraceptive device (IUD) functions by preventing implantation of fertilized eggs in the uterus, the woman using one would be guilty of an ongoing series of murders of American citizens. Her IUD would be an illegal lethal weapon. A search of a woman's womb would be in order if there is some evidence that she is sexually active and carrying a citizen-killer. A pregnant woman who attempts to have an illegal abortion could be incarcerated or trailed by undercover agents, since she would have shown murderous intentions.

The more you stretch an idea that is fundamentally absurd, the more its nonsense emerges. In other words, the truth washes; error does not. The whole federal bureaucracy—so abhorred by the New Right—would have to grow enormously to provide for the "million unseen citizens." It has been pointed out, in opposition to the Human Life Amendment, that since 11 million fertilized eggs come into existence each year, census taking becomes a problem, as does the apportionment of representation in each state. New census forms would have to be developed, since we would not know—without amniocentesis—the sex of these intrauterine "citizens." Would a fetus need a passport? Would a child conceived abroad but born in the United States be an alien?[21] Would a child of citizens of another country who was conceived in this country while the parents were traveling here be considered a citizen of the United States? These very questions suggest that something silly is afoot. Something sinister is also afoot, since government would be invited in a whole new dimension into the private matter of pregnancy. That is not a profamily prospect.

The Perils of Patriarchy

Notice again the connection between the New Right's interest in the family and their goal of a different kind of political society.

They see the family as the basis and bedrock of the state; it is also the model of the state. Their family model and their government model are patriarchal. A good, strong, Christian father would not let his wife go off and abort his child. However, in the view of the New Right, he has a problem. Women have been beguiled by humanistic and socialist ideas, and it is getting harder to keep them in tow. Ideally, fathers could by themselves, control their wives and daughters with just a little help from the male clergy. Senator Laxalt granted this idea in introducing his Family Protection Act. But then he went on to acknowledge that these are not the best of times. Therefore, the government has to get into the act. The threats to the family are such as to require "a political defense." [22] Government has to act like a strong "Christian" father. This is a theory of government *in loco patris*. If a strong Christian father at home cannot stop abortions, the backup "Christian father"—government—will. If the father cannot root out all the ideas in the schools that offend "Christian," New Right conservatives, the government will. If wives run away from their "Christian" husbands, the government will limit the facilities for battered women that provide refuge. If the "Christian" father cannot get his children into a "Christian" indoctrination school, the government will make sure that they say their prayers in the public school, and get appropriately spanked. The family formula for the New Right is patriarchal. For them, paternal authority is fascistic, narrow, stern, authoritarian, and muscular. This provides a model for an increasingly fascistic state.

Sexism as a Social Disease

The New Right's crusade for the family is at its root an effort to return to pure patriarchy, which is the symptom of a deeper and more pervasive malady—sexism. Sexism imports a belief in the inferiority of women. Sexism is a foundational perversion and the elementary sin. We are all afflicted with it to some degree, since it pervades history in such a way that none is untouched by its pernicious influence. In the New Right, sexism is in full bloom. For this reason their purported love of family is spurious.

For all the talk about sexism, the depth of its malignant influence on culture, economy, religion, education, and self-understanding is too rarely taken seriously. As the New Right family and the New Right "Christian" school are workshops for the reinforcement of sexism, it would be difficult to overestimate the amount of evil they can do.

Sexism perverts our notion of humanity. The human essence is dyadic, male and female. To pervert one part is to pervert the other. To distort femininity and masculinity, the basic ingredients of humanity, is to distort humanity. Nothing will be spared the fallout from this deep perversion. This is "original sin." All human ideas, customs, and institutions bear the mark of this fundamental corruption. The solution, of course, does not mean the triumph of the feminine over the masculine. Ideally, the two could blend into a richer humanity. At the moment, a distorted masculinity dominates society. And it is this distortion that the New Right supports with all its vigor. In so doing, they contribute to the corruption not only of the family, but of all our social institutions.

The culprit is macho-masculinity. Not all women are good and not all men are bad. Men, however, are in charge, and dominate positions of power and privilege in both church and state. They enjoy monopolies in the realms of finance, education, and almost all the professions. In the pulpit, state house, and board room they preside. How have centuries of domination affected the dominators? To answer these questions, we have to run the danger of stereotyping. If there is some reality that attaches to the term "macho-masculinity"—and I submit that there is—it must be stated that not all men have it to the same degree, and that not all women lack it. There are, however, qualities that attach to male-dominated institutions that can be discerned. The macho male is not pure myth. He exists and his influence on the institutions he dominates must be identified and remedied if humanity is to strive to heal itself from its radical male/female split.

It is a blunt historical fact, with only exceptions here and there, that men have been the warriors of the race. They left nurturing women in the cave and, in facing a resistant world outside, struggled against nature and their own kind. The struggle shaped them and gave them their worldviews. It also left them, and us, with some pervasive pathologies. There are four salient aspects to macho-masculinity that can be observed: 1) aggression and a proneness to violent solutions; 2) a penchant for hierarchical rather than cooperative models; 3) a tendency to indulge in abstractions that obscure the facts; and 4) a debilitating hatred of women. Not every man in every culture has all these negative traits, and not to the same degree. But, I would argue, where discernibly macho-masculinity appears, these will be the visible markings of it.

Violence

The Amazons are mythic creatures; war has been a male preserve. And the kind of courage that has been held in highest esteem is mainly the courage of the warrior. Has this fact of history entered into human life? Are there any clues that male-dominated institutions and systems are geared to bellicosity? There is one not at all subtle clue. It is estimated that the overwhelmingly male-dominated nations of the world spend at least one million dollars a minute on preparations for war (arbitrarily called "defense"). However, war and preparation for war do not exhaust the possibilities of bellicosity. Warriors, fortunately, do not always find wars to fight in. The military mindset can also translate into nonwarring forms of aggression in other areas of life. The macho-masculine approach to life tends to be aggressive, rather than caring, engendering, and relational.

Metaphors are revealing. In the masculine world, problems are *assaulted*, not solved. Diseases are *defeated*, not cured. A *killing* is made in the market. The Christian cross is a *triumph*, and God a *mighty fortress*. The system is to be *beaten*, and the *frontiers* of knowledge *pushed back*. Even gentle poetry has been called a *raid* on the inarticulate. A good personality is a *winning* personality.

Our games as well as our metaphors show what we are. An ancient axiom says that it is at play that we most reveal our moral orientation (*Inter ludendum mores se detegunt*). A look at a National Football League game, and at the names of the teams competing in that league, gives a grim portrait of the American male at play. Aggression, not harmony, is supreme in a male-dominated world. The impact of this on religion, mores, and learning is not slight. The infection penetrates the roots of everything in society.

For example, when the warrior male goes into business, business is an arena for war. Competition takes on a ruthless ferocity. Businessmen speak admiringly of one another as "sharks." In the United States, business is aggression. In the language of the hunt, you must "corner the market," "wipe out" the competition and see that the bull displaces the bear. Small businessmen, willing or not, are swallowed by the bigger ones. The shark, after all, does not invite you to dinner; you *are* dinner. The inefficient or the aged are fired. Aged warriors are dispensable. The admittedly "gentler sex" does not get into management. The marketplace becomes a heartless zone.

Macho America is belatedly taking notice of Japanese business. Though Japan is by no means free of macho-masculinity, in comparison its business world follows a more feminine model. Japanese workers, even those who prove to be less efficient, are tenured and retrained. (A mother would not throw a child out for inefficiency in the home.) Labor, government, and management work together in what has been called a "corporate model of cooperative nationhood." Accommodation and patience mark their dealings. There is no effort to get one "off the back" of the other, as in the controversy model of American life. Japan, with half of our population, has only 11,000 lawyers, while we have 415,000. Conflict resolution is more sophisticated, and does not regularly descend into litigation wars, as it is with knee-jerk regularity in this country. It is redemptive for the American male to finally notice that the Japanese feminine model is also more productive.

Hierarchy

Connected to the aggressive approach to challenges is the hierarchical instinct. Violence and aggression do not seek cooperation, but dominance, which, of course, is the antithesis of *friendship* and *community*, both of which are based on mutuality and harmony. Hence, the male tendency in state, church, corporation, and family is toward hierarchy and control, rather than communion. Hierarchy is also divisive. It involves the subordination of some to others, and subordination separates. This affects, for example, the male-dominated academic world. Domination and triumph, rather than a quiet seeking and waiting for truth, mark the masculine world of scholars. The "clubbing" or pack instinct pits groups and disciplines against one another. Disciplines become beleaguered and fortified enclaves. They stand against one another like isolated and hostile units, sealed off by passwords or jargon unknown to the outsider.

The same spirit infects male-dominated churches, which multiply and divide. Efforts at ecumenism are tentative, hedged, and most often merely liturgical. Separateness, defensiveness, and implicit hostility are accepted as normal, though there are no ultimate theological grounds for division at all. In the international order, patterns of cooperation and sharing among the sovereign nation-states are feeble and mistrusted. The right's horror of the United Nations illustrates this.

All these sins of division cannot be ascribed simply to masculinity. Simplistic answers are always suspect in complex human affairs. Nevertheless, the behavior involved is quite congenial to the macho-masculine mode of living. It is not too much to suggest that a humanity that is not split against itself at its dyadic, male/female roots would do things differently.

Abstractions over Facts

The greatest evil, said Sartre, is to treat as abstract that which is concrete. The male mind has a weakness for doing just that.

Only a man, one might dare say, could stand in the ashes of the obliterated village of Ben Tre during the Vietnam war and say, as a Colonel did: "We had to destroy this village in order to save it." Feminine experience makes women less likely to miss the disconnection between ashen destruction and *saving*. Helium-filled abstractions like "national security," "national interest," and "nuclear superiority," can mesmerize the male mind, to the undoing of all concrete meaning of "security," "interest," and "superiority." Such a lethal distraction is harder for woman. She is closer in her historical experience and socialization to the flesh and to the earth in which all value resides. A man can speak more easily of *"acceptable* levels of unemployment."

The abstractionist tendencies of the male relate to the inherent violence in male-dominated affairs. Violence requires abstracting. If we do not, in anger, abstract from the humanity, vulnerability, kinship, and similarity of our enemy, our zeal for battle evanesces. The abstractionist tendency of the male, like his proneness to violence, also relates to the tasks that were heaped on him historically. He was the one who had to leave the redeeming presence of children and go out to plow, hunt, and achieve in a resistant and threatening world. The male perforce has been task-oriented. To be task-oriented is to be future-oriented. The prize of the struggle is not yet attained. Thus, a hard-working man can sacrifice any real contact or friendship with his wife or children because he is working so hard to make their futures secure. This devastates the person of the man. Yet this is the "work ethic" so lauded by the Falwells and the LaHayes. The perfect specimen of the work ethic is the workaholic, who has no time for ecstasy or delight in the present. He is consumed by his future goals and plans. It is sobering to note the growing number of women who are millionaires, but who did not work for their money outside the home. They are widows of successful men who followed the logic of their vision to their graves. The work ethic, as it is championed and lived in this nation, is not profamily. To be forced into "making it" in a world of warriors is dangerous to one's health. It is the masculine, more than the feminine, that needs liberation. The New Right men have no sense of this.

Hatred of Women

Hatred is, admittedly, a strong word. Too emotive, perhaps? An unhelpful rhetorical indulgence? No. Hatred is, sadly, the perfect word for the macho attitude toward women. But how does one go about hating those whom we put on pedestals and in centerfolds, and with whom we share both bed and board? The answer is: complicatedly.

Hatred is sustained anger and disdain. If anger is a transient emotion, hatred is tenured anger. It is marked by aversion and degradation. One mark of an operative hatred is exclusion; the form that sustained exclusion takes is monopoly. In the United States, for two hundred years, we have operated on a rigid quota system that insists on and has a 90 to 100 percent monopoly of white males in all the centers of power in government, business, and the professions, and in the competition for desirable jobs at every level.[23] The success of this monopolistic venture could be due to only one of two things: either males deserve this status and have, like cream, risen to the top, or, an effective, multileveled monopoly has excluded women from many desirable areas of life, relegating them to more menial and subservient positions. The male ego might prefer the first explanation, but it has little to support it.

A monopoly is hostile and egoistic. It implies the superiority of the monopolizers and the inferiority of the excluded. The more comfortable the monopolizers are, the more deep-seated is their disdain. If they are uneasy with the privileges they have arrogated to themselves, it would imply some recognition on their part of unduly excluded value in the banished persons. The American monopoly is comfortably in place, and even the slight efforts to challenge it, like the Equal Rights Amendment and the affirmative action programs, are being successfully resisted. Hatred is a fair name for this phenomenon.

The disabling aversion to women also affects religion. Both Judaism and Christianity are quite fixated on the maleness of God. This, of course, is a gratuitous assumption. Religious ideas arise when persons look at themselves and the world around them. They see the bird in flight, the rose in bloom, and the infant blessing us with smiles, and they utter the primal expression of religious consciousness: "There is more to this than meets the eye." The religious inference here is that deep down inside observable reality is a creative presence, a directing force, which underlies the complexities and the beauties of the natural setting. This presence is then named God. To infer the reality of this presence, and then go on to say it must be male, is a baffling step. Identifying the gender of the presence might be of some symbolic helpfulness, but assignating a clearly exclusionary maleness is utterly arbitrary. In fact, the fruitful maternal womb, seems a more promising image of the divinity, and many world religions have chosen that image. Yet, there are limits even to a maternal imagery. God is always beyond the reach of our symbols.

When one alleges that God, the Ground of all Being, is male, then male chauvinism is absolute, since it conditions all that is. All that is would be made in the image of the masculine. By insisting on the masculinity of God, Judaism and Christianity in all its forms make quite a few negative statements about women and their dignity. Beyond that, many religions insist on an all-male clergy. No theological purpose for this can be given. (The penis serves no religious or other purpose in the sanctuary or at the altar.) Roman Catholicism even goes one step further than other male-dominated religions by insisting that the male priest be celibate. A man contaminated by marriage to a woman may not preside at Catholic worship. However mandatory celibacy for priests is rationalized, it looms symbolically as an institutionalized aversion to woman. The fact that the Catholic Church will close down parishes for lack of priests and will leave "mission areas" without priests for indefinite long periods, sooner than permit women or married men to minister, bespeaks an indentured sexism.

Sexism is a serious sickness. It poisons our attitudes toward women, and toward all that is associated with them. The New Right is a living museum of sexism. The family they want is a sexist shrine where the authority (superiority) of the male is the cornerstone, set there by God *him*self. They would purge our schools and libraries of all that touches on the liberation of woman from their inferior image. Women are viewed as a hostile force, threatening the various male domains. Jerry Falwell uses a very significant verb to describe the movement of women into the world. He laments that from astronauts to zoologists, almost every occupation has been "invaded" by women.[24] The "invaders" must be sent back to the hearth that is their destiny.

The New Right does well to worry about the stability of homes and families, and the increasingly quaint way in which people look on commitment and fidelity. Their prescription, however, will not work. A woman has a right to be a mother and a housewife, and, similarly, a man has a right to be a father and a househusband. But she has many other rights and talents also, which must be allowed to flower. Care for children must be more broadly shared, so that the human family will no longer be deprived of the God-given talents of women in all areas of life. If the New Right were profamily, and not just pro-male control of family and everything else, they would champion the idea of paternity leave for fathers, equal pay for women, daycare centers, shared child care, language lessons for immigrant families, and most of all, a return to sanity in military expenditures. Military expenditure is the principal cause of inflation, which is the most antifamily reality in our lives. The sacred cow of militarism is the beast that kills families, even if it does not get a chance to actually go to war. If the New Right were profamily, they would also promote harmony between labor, government, and business, instead of supporting aggressive relations among these three natural partners in any economy.

The biggest family challenge is to take men off the backs of women, so that from child care to engineering, from governing to scientific research, from home building to world building, we might join one another in work that is, at last, fully human.

A Note on Homosexuality

One of the most remarkable passions of the New Right is their anti-homosexuality. Their expression of an abhorrence of homosexuality reaches heights of fervor. That fervor finds its way into the Family Protection Act in what amounts to a call for the legitimation of discrimination. The act proposes an amendment to the Civil Rights Act of 1964 that would deprive homosexual citizens of their civil liberty. As an example of brute prejudice trying to work its way into law, the language of the act merits full quotation: "As used in the Act, the term 'unlawful employment practice' shall not be deemed to include any action or measure taken by an employer, labor organization, joint labor-management committee, or employment agency with respect to an individual who is a homosexual or proclaims homosexual tendencies. No agency, bureau, commission or other instrumentality of the Government of the United States shall seek to enforce nondiscrimination with respect to individuals who are homosexuals or who proclaim homosexual tendencies."[25] Federal funds would also be forbidden to any agency that provides legal assistance in any proceeding or litigation regarding "the issue of gay rights."[26]

Estimates vary, but it is commonly estimated that at least 4 or 5 percent of American citizens are homosexually oriented. This comprises some ten million people—all of whom would be deprived of protection against discrimination if their sexual orientation became known. Many societies viewed homosexuality with indifference or with a quiet tolerance. Our society is not that way, but is marked by an extremely negative attitude toward homosexuality. This means that homosexuals are likely to feel the weight of that attitude in their educational, employment, and housing situations. Efforts at a redress of this situation would be taken away by the legislation supported by the New Right.

Again we see the historical and biblical ignorance of the New Right about homosexuality. They misinterpret biblical texts, ignore their archaic cultic preoccupations and primitive psychology, and instead read into "Christian" history a unanimous tirade against homosexuality. There was the indentured magical interpretation of the Sodom story which left early Christians with the impression that God was so offended by homosexual practices that He destroyed their cities. In spite of this horrid prospect, homosexuality was not such an obsession for the early Christians as it is for the New Right Christians. As one Catholic study put it: "Official Church teaching and legislation is not wanting regarding homosexual practice, beginning as early as the fourth century with the Council of Elvira. It is surprising, however, that the condemnations are relatively few and sporadic. The Church has commonly been accused of sustaining an unrelenting persecution of homosexuals. Careful study of the historical documents indicates nothing of the kind. One finds councils and synods denouncing sodomy from time to time, but invariably in conjunction with other carnal sins. Homosexuals are rarely singled out for special hostility."[27]

In a recent and most thorough historical study of Christian attitudes toward homosexuality, John Boswell points out that a tradition of remarkable tolerance of minority experiences underwent an abrupt change in the later Middle Ages. He rejects the misuse of the term "medieval" as meaning intolerant, oppressive, and narrow-minded, since in the Early Middle Ages, this was not the case. He notes, for example, that for the most part "Jews and gay people not only lived quietly among the general population but often rose to positions of prominence and power."[28] His connecting of Jews and homosexuals is significant because, as tolerance broke down toward the end of the twelfth century, inimical feelings and persecution broke out against Jews, homosexuals, and other minorities, who began to learn then what majority intolerance can mean. A sense of history would show the New Right that they are the sequel to a paranoid and cruel turn in late medieval history. It would also show them something else: their preoccupation is with male homosexuality, which is consistent with the historical form of Christianity that they represent. As one study points out: there is an anomaly within the Christian tradition regarding homosexuality.

"The medieval penitentials, Church legislation and Christian tradition in general penalize homosexual acts by men with uncommon severity, while virtually disregarding those by women." The authors conclude that the explanation seems to lie "in the sexist androcentrism of the West and a reverence for semen that borders on superstition."[29] The profound sexism of the rightists clearly enters into their condemnation of homosexuality. The homosexual male is perceived as a womanized male. The incarnation of feminine inferiority in a male is especially repugnant. The gay male is a threat to macho-masculinity. Hence the colossal animus toward male homosexuals.

Another problem with the New Right regarding homosexuals is that they are as innocent of psychology as they are of history. Falwell tells us apodictically that no one is born gay. Persons are seduced into homosexuality by rapacious gays who also want to reproduce their own sordid perversion in our children. Since homosexuals do not reproduce children, they have to recruit them, Falwell tells us.[30] New Right writings show ignorance of the extensive studies of the origins of homosexuality. Their simplistic view is that it only takes one quaff of a conversion potion to turn a homosexual into a heterosexual. Their conclusion in this crude psychology is that all homosexuals are guilty of a contumacious violation of their God-given heterosexuality. They are also guilty of seductive intentions toward our children. Thus, given their power to lure children—and given their need to do so because their sexual activity does not fulfill their desire for progeny—there is no reason why federal funds should be used to defend their rights. There is also no reason why schools who fire them, or landlords who evict them, should be prosecuted for discrimination. Acting in self-protection is not discrimination. That is the cruel logic of the New Right, and is in the spirit of the Code of Theodosius and the Code of Justinian, which proscribed homosexual activity under pain of death by fire. At least the New Right doesn't go that far. They will settle for legalized discrimination.

The subject of homosexuality is difficult to deal with in American culture. There are too many myths born of ignorance and fear. Also, as one study states: ". . . for people not altogether secure in their own sexual identity, homosexuality is a highly emotional subject, not easily permitting of concrete objective discussion."[31] Violence against homosexuals is increasing in our time. The New Right is responsible for infusing new doses of prejudice and hatred into the discriminatory atmosphere that already exists. It has never been shown that homosexuals are more prone to sexual harassment and seduction of others than heterosexuals. Indeed, the truth about sexual harassment by heterosexuals on the job and in schools is just beginning to emerge. In times past, women and girls were in a difficult position to press charges, and were not socialized to expect success in bringing private harassment to the attention of male managers and school principals. Whereas harassment by homosexuals is page-one news, harassment by heterosexual males is unreported by the male-dominated media. Any sexual harassment is a form of rape, an execrable abuse. But when a white male movement such as the New Right tries to paint it as the peculiar penchant of homosexuals, their position offends both justice and truth.

It is the way of subversives to say one thing and mean another. The New Right's "family" interests actually takes us far from the hearth. It reveals a political plan to dominate women and children. It allows government control of the womb. It excommunicates some ten million homosexual citizens from their civil rights. It perverts the notion of majority rule in the democratic process. It points us toward the model of a fascist family in a fascist state. And all this in the blessed name of "family."

Conclusion:
ON A NOTE OF HOPE

G.K.Chesterton claimed that the majority is always wrong. The founding fathers of this nation knew that the majority could be wrong, and so they tempered majority rule with a concern for minorities. The Moral Majority, and its brother groups, are clearly wrong about one thing. They are not a majority. They do not even represent a majority of those who call themselves Christian. As the Baptist minister Howard Hartzell has stressed against the Falwellians, the Baptist ideal has always been to be a *humble minority* struggling to give witness to gospel values.[1] The Moral Majoritarians have, however, demonstrated the power to summon majority votes in a number of instances. Exploiting fears, uncertainties, single-issue passions, and voter apathy, they can make a considerable impact, and have already done so. And unless the "rapture" arrives and spirits them away from us, they will be here for the foreseeable future. How then might I speak of hope?

First of all, it is clear that publicity is not a blessing for the New Right. The best defense against them is exposure. They are getting exposed. From creationist trials to talk shows, they are in the public eye, and people are understanding the threat. The New Right has also become defensive. The Moral Majority takes full-page ads in major newspapers to counter the "charges" against them. In the process they moderate their opinions a little. Falwell is notorious for backtracking when under fire.

And most remarkably, self-criticism has entered the ranks of the deviant fundamentalists—a most promising augury. As of this writing, in the newest book from the Falwell pen, he and his fundamentalist coauthors offer some serious criticism of the New Right movement. Their examination of their fundamentalist consciences yields these admissions. They accept blame for having too little capacity for self-criticism. As a result, they say, fundamentalists are "overly defensive and ingrown." Fundamentalists, they concede, must refrain from blasting everyone who offers even slight disagreement with them.[2] They admit to being fixated on external piety. They worry about smoking and drinking, but are themselves often bitter, hostile, and unloving. They see that they need more balance.[3] They admit that fundamentalists have been too resistant to change.[4]

They go on to accuse themselves of elevating minor matters over the "weightier matters" of the law.[5] They say they have made up parts of the gospel. They allow that preaching on "the evils of evolution" has its place in fundamentalism, but that it is not the message of the gospel. They also admit the tendency in fundamentalist preaching to be *against* many things rather than to be *for* the central message of Jesus.[6] They admit, too, to the development of a "paranoid mentality" toward the world they are trying to reach. They also say that fundamentalists rarely practice what they preach on racial justice.[7] They criticize their own "overabsolutism," the tendency to see things as absolutely right or absolutely wrong. And finally, they criticize their claim that "they alone are saved."[8] Certainly all these concessions in one way or another are points that those of us outside fundamentalism have been trying to make. To read them in a book written by three fundamentalists, one of whom is Jerry Falwell, is indeed progress. How widely influential these concessions will be in the movement is another matter. Still, it does indicate that, at least at Liberty Baptist College in Virginia, some of the root problems of aberrant fundamentalism are surfacing.

There is another sign of hope. People are organizing in response to the fundamentalist onslaught. Former Senator George Mc-

Govern has founded a national organization, Americans for Common Sense, to react to New Right propaganda by appealing to those basic human values that hold the pluralistic American society together.[9] Norman Lear and others have founded People for the American Way.[10] Like Americans for Common Sense, Lear's group has a varied program, and is seeking creative responses to the real problem areas addressed so strangely by the New Right. At the initiative of Rabbi Francis Barry Silberg, another national group, Moral Alternatives, has been founded.[11] This group, which includes on its national board some of the principal religious scholars in the country, wishes to address the distortions of religious categories by the new Christian right.

None of these groups is infallible, nor do any of them have an income comparable to that of the gilded operations of the New Right. They do represent hope, however. It is to be fervently wished that they also represent a trend. The old coalitions for social justice and for the cohesive and unitive values of American life have weakened. If New Right extremism inspires political counterorganization, then born-again deviant fundamentalism will have proved itself a saving grace.

In these pages I have spoken directly, and at times harshly, of the problems of the New Right. I believe that nothing less will do. The New Rightists come to us with smiles and unctuous righteousness, hiding their mean purposes under biblical and patriotic guises. Even if it seems impolite to do so, the reality they represent must be faced and called to task. These people are not simply one more fair-minded interest group making its way in the world of politics. They are subversives. Their programs offend both religion and the cause of political peace and justice. The power that thrills them must alert us to their danger. The economic situation in this country is tightening, and therefore opportunities for New Right mischief are improving. The price of indifference to this troublesome force will be high.

Notes

Chapter One

1. Allan J. Mayer et al., "A Tide of Born-Again Politics," *Newsweek*, September 15, 1980, p. 29.

2. Richard A. Viguerie, *The New Right: We're Ready to Lead* (Falls Church, Virginia: The Viguerie Co., 1981).

3. Richard Hofstadter, *The Paranoid Style in American Politics and Other Essays* (New York: Alfred A. Knopf, 1965), p. 32.

4. Carl Bode, ed., *The New Mencken Letters* (New York: The Dial Press, 1977), p. 187.

5. H.L. Mencken, *A Mencken Chrestomathy* (New York: Alfred A. Knopf, 1974), p. 398.

6. Jerry Falwell, with Ed Dobson and Ed Hindson, *The Fundamentalist Phenomenon: Resurgence of Conservative Christianity* (Garden City, New York: Doubleday & Co., 1981), p. 132.

7. Quoted by Martin E. Marty, "Things Fall Apart," in *The Christian Century* 97, September 10–17, 1980, p. 863.

8. Quoted ibid.

9. Ibid.

10. Andy Pasztor, "James Watt: Land is his Mission," reprinted in *The Boston Globe*, May 6, 1981.

11. Quoted in Richard A. Viguerie, *The New Right*, p. 56.

12. Richard Hofstadter, *The Paranoid Style in American Politics*, pp. 43–44.

13. Theodore W. Adorno et al., *The Authoritarian Personality* (New York: Harper, 1950), p. 676.

14. Richard Hofstadter, *The Paranoid Style in American Politics*, p. 47.

15. Irving R. Kaufman, "Congress v. the Court," *The New York Times Magazine*, September 20, 1981, p. 44.

16. Jefferson's *Bill for Establishing Religious Freedom in Virginia*, introduced in 1779, passed in 1786. Quoted in J.M. O'Neill, *Religion and Education Under the Constitution* (New York: Harper & Brothers, 1949), p. 275.

17. Ibid.

18. Ibid., p. 276.

19. Jerry Falwell, *Listen America!* (New York: Bantam Books, 1980), p. 25. Emphasis added.

20. Ibid., p. 53.

21. Jerry Falwell, *Listen America!* p. 12.

22. J.M. O'Neill, *Religion and Education Under the Constitution*, p. 19.

23. Hal Lindsay with C.C. Carlson, *The Late Great Planet Earth* (New York: Bantam Books, 1973), p. ii.

24. "Evangelist Reverses Position on God Hearing Jews," *The Washington Post*, October 11, 1980.

25. Richard Viguerie, *The New Right*, p. 190.

26. Jerry Falwell, *How You Can Help Clean Up America* (Lynchburg, Virginia: Liberty Publishing Co., 1978), p. 19.

27. Jerry Falwell, *Listen America!*, p. 159.

28. Ibid., p. 92.

29. Cullen Murphy, "Protestantism and the Evangelicals," *The Wilson Quarterly* 5, Autumn 1981, p. 106.

30. George M. Marsden, *Fundamentalism and American Culture: The Shaping of Twentieth Century Evangelicalism: 1870–1925* (New York/Oxford: Oxford University Press, 1980), p. 4.

31. Jim Wallis, "Recovering the Evangel," *Sojourners*, February 1981, p. 3.

32. Billy Graham, "A Change of Heart," *Sojourners*, August 1978.

33. John C. Bennett, "Assessing the Concerns of the Religious Right," *The Christian Century*, October 14, 1981, p. 1022.

34. Martin E. Marty, "Twelve Points to Consider," *Face to Face: An Interreligious Bulletin* 8, Winter 1981, p. 17.

35. Quoted in Richard V. Pierard, "An Innocent in Babylon," *The Christian Century*, February 27, 1980, p. 191.

36. David Edwin Harrell, Jr., "The Roots of the Moral Majority: Fundamentalism Revisited," *Occasional Papers* 15, May 1981, p. 11.

37. Richard V. Pierard, "An Innocent in Babylon," p. 191.

38. Philip Yancey, "The Ironies and Impact of PTL," *Christianity Today*, September 21, 1979, p. 32.

39. Robert McAfee Brown, "The Need for a Moral Minority," *Face to Face* 8, Winter 1981, p. 14. For an informed, informing, and balanced view of the religious and political significance of the New Right, see Peggy L. Shriver, *The Bible Vote: Religion and the New Right* (New York: The Pilgrim Press, 1981).

Chapter Two

1. Richard Hofstadter, *The Paranoid Style in American Politics*, p. 65.

2. Ibid., p. xii.

3. Editorial, "Vanishing Fundamentalism," *The Christian Century* 43, June 24, 1926, p. 799.

4. Cullen Murphy, "Protestantism and the Evangelicals," p. 107.

5. Huston Smith, *The Religions of Man* (New York: Harper & Row, Perennial Library, 1965), p. 11.

6. Arnold J. Toynbee, *Change and Habit* (New York and London: Oxford University Press, 1966), p. 104.

7. Ibid., p. 106.

8. Ibid., p. 107.

9. Ibid., p. 110.

10. Jerry Falwell, *Listen, America!* p. 43. Tim LaHaye, *The Battle For the Mind* (Old Tappan, New Jersey: Fleming H. Revell Co., Power Books, 1980), p. 37.

11. George S. Phillips, *The American Republic and Human Liberty Foreshadowed in Scripture* (Cincinnati: Poe and Hitchcock, 1864).

12. William A. Clebsch, *From Sacred to Profane America: The Role of Religion in American History* (New York, Evanston, and London: Harper & Row, 1968), pp. 191–192.

13. George S. Phillips, *The American Republic*, pp. 130, 153.

14. Jerry Falwell et al., *The Fundamentalist Phenomenon*, pp. 182–183.

15. George M. Marsden, *Fundamentalism and American Culture*, p. 119.

16. Richard Hofstadter, *Anti-Intellectualism in American Life* (New York: Alfred A. Knopf, 1970), p. 121.

17. On the imagery of the involuntary immigrants, see George Marsden, *Fundamentalism and American Culture*, pp. 204–205.

18. I owe this information to Falwell's book, *The Fundamentalist Phenomenon*, p. 180.

19. Richard Hofstadter, *The Paranoid Style in American Politics*, p. 39.

20. Martin E. Marty, *Righteous Empire: The Protestant Experience in America* (New York: The Dial Press, 1970), p. 24.

21. Richard H. de Lone, *Small Futures: Children, Inequality and the Limits of Liberal Reform* (New York and London: Harcourt Brace Jovanovich, 1977), p. 7.

22. Tim LaHaye, *The Battle For the Mind*, pp. 213–214.

23. Quoted in *Time*, June 8, 1981, p. 55.

24. See Gerald R. Gill, *Meanness Mania: The Changed Mood* (Washington, D.C.: Howard University Press, 1980). Gill is not referring narrowly to the new Christian right in his book, but his message applies to them in all respects.

25. Quoted in Gerry O'Sullivan, "Voting for God," *Point* 10, October 1980, p. 7.

26. Rosemary Ruether, "Politics and the Family: Recapturing a Lost Issue," *Christianity and Crisis*, September 29, 1980, p. 266.

27. Douglas Sloan, "The Teaching of Ethics in the American Undergraduate Curriculum, 1876–1976," *Ethics Teaching in Higher Education*, Daniel Callahan and Sissela Bok, eds. (New York and London: Plenum Press, 1980), p. 2.

28. Ibid., p. 9.

29. Quoted ibid., note 16.

30. Robert J. Baum, *Ethics and Engineering Curricula* (Hastings-on-Hudson, New York: The Hastings Center, 1980), pp. 11–13.

31. Quoted in *Time* (June 8, 1981), p. 54.
32. Quoted ibid.
33. Jerry Falwell, *Listen, America!* p. 173.

Chapter Three
1. Jerry Falwell, *Listen, America!* p. 19.
2. Ibid., p. 54.
3. Tim LaHaye, *The Battle For the Mind*, pp. 218, 241–242.
4. Jerry Falwell, *Listen, America!* pp. 97–98.
5. Hal Lindsey, with C.C. Carlson, *The Late Great Planet Earth*, p. 99.
6. Allan J. Mayer et al., "A Tide of Born-Again Politics," *Newsweek*, September 15, 1980, p. 36.
7. Marsden, *Fundamentalism and American Culture*, p. 217.
8. Quoted ibid., pp. 217–18.
9. Charles Blanchard, *Method in Biblical Criticism*, cited in Marsden, *Fundamentalism and American Culture*, p. 220.
10. Ibid.
11. Quoted in David Edwin Harrell, Jr., "The Roots of the Moral Majority," p. 8.
12. Quoted in Marsden, *Fundamentalism and American Culture*, p. 130.
13. Quoted in Richard Hofstadter, *Anti-Intellectualism in American Life*, p. 122.
14. Quoted in Marsden, *Fundamentalism and American Culture*, p. 212.
15. Quoted ibid., p. 4.
16. Alice Kehoe, "Scientific Creationism," in Laurie Godfrey, ed., *A Century After Darwin* (New York: Allyn & Bacon, 1982).
17. Niles Eldredge, "Creationism Isn't Science," *The New Republic* 184, April 4, 1981, p. 15.
18. See 393 *US* at 101 and 393 *US* at 103.
19. See *Daniel v. Water*, 515 F. 2d. 485 (1975).
20. Tim LaHaye, *The Battle For the Mind*, p. 50.
21. Ibid.
22. Professor Dean R. Fowler, Marquette University, developed this report on creationist activities in an excellent paper, "The Creationist Movement," and he graciously gave me a copy of it prior to its publication.
23. Tim LaHaye, *The Battle For the Mind*, p. 50.
24. *The Jerusalem Bible* (Garden City, New York: Doubleday, 1966), p. 15, note 1a.
25. Ibid.
26. Niles Eldredge, "Creationism Isn't Science," pp. 15, 16.
27. Tim LaHaye, *The Battle For the Mind*, p. 51.
28. Teilhard de Chardin, *The Phenomenon of Man* (New York: Harper and Row, Harper Torchbook, 1961), p. 218.
29. Quoted in Marsden, *Fundamentalism and American Culture*, p. 209.
30. For this letter, I am indebted to Reverend Howard Hartzell, who brought it

to my attention, and to Reverend Gordon Poteat and Reverend Lilburn Mosely, who permitted me to include it in these pages.

31. Stephen Charles Mott, "Egalitarian Aspects of the Biblical Theory of Justice," *Selected Papers, 1978: The American Society of Christian Ethics* (Waterloo, Canada: Wilfred Laurier University, 1978), p. 8.

32. Norman H. Snaith, *The Distinctive Ideas of the Old Testament* (London: The Epworth Press, 1962), pp. 71–72.

33. Ibid., pp. 68–70.

34. Stephen Charles Mott, *Egalitian Aspects*, p. 15.

35. Robert McAfee Brown, "Listen, Jerry Falwell!" *Christianity and Crisis*, December 22, 1980, p. 361.

36. William F. Fore, "Forms of Self-Deception and Hypocrisy," *The Christian Century* 97, October 22, 1980, p. 1004.

37. "Christian Theological Observations on the Religious Right: A Statement by 15 American Church Bodies," *Face to Face: An Interreligious Bulletin* 8, Winter 1981, pp. 6–7. The statement is signed by representatives of the following churches: Methodist, Lutheran, Baptist, Methodist Episcopal, Evangelical Covenant Church, Friends General Conference, Church of the Brethren, United Church of Christ, Disciples of Christ, and Presbyterian.

38. Donald W. Shriver, Jr., "The Temptation of Self-Righteousness," *The Christian Century* 97, October 22, 1980, p. 1002.

Chapter Four

1. See Martin E. Marty, *Righteous Empire: The Protestant Experience in America*, pp. 38–39.

2. Ibid., p. 39.

3. Origen, *Works*, Berlin Corpus, vol. 11, pp. 221–222.

4. See Stanley Windass, *Christianity Versus Violence: A Social and Historical Study of War and Christianity* (London: Sheed and Ward, 1964), p. 13.

5. *Inst.* IV, XX, 15–17.

6. *Inst.* VI, 20.

7. Minucius Felix, Oct. XXX, 6.

8. Quoted in Origen, *Contra Celsum*, VIII, 68–69.

9. Ibid.

9a. Eusebius, *Vita Constantini* 1, 24.

10. Lactantius, *Institute* vii. 26.

11. Eusebius, *Vita Constantini* 2, 28–29.

12. Ibid., pp. 2, 55.

13. Paneg. 2.

14. Theodoret., *Hist. Eccl.* II, 26.

15. Theodosian Code, xvi, x, 21.

16. Augustine, *De Libero Arbitrio*, Migne, *Patres Latini* 32, 1227–1228.

17. Augustine, *Contra Faustum*, Migne, *Patres Latini*, 42, 449.

18. Augustine, *Epist.* 138, ii, 14.

19. See Roland Bainton, *Christian Attitudes Toward War and Peace: A Historical*

Survey and Critical Re-evaluation (New York, Nashville: Abingdon Press, 1960), pp. 101–111.

20. See *Dictionnaire de Theologie Catholique*, vol. VI, col. 1920.

21. Quoted in Roland Bainton, *Christian Attitudes Toward War and Peace*, p. 110.

22. Stanley Windass, *Christianity Versus Violence*, p. 43.

23. *Calvini opera*, in *Corpus Reformatorum*, VIII, 476; XXIV, 360; XLIV, 346.

24. Roland Bainton, *Christian Attitudes Toward War and Peace*, pp. 112–13.

25. Ibid., p. 112.

26. Ibid., p. 115.

27. Jerry Falwell et al., *The Fundamentalist Phenomenon*, p. 75.

28. See George Marsden, *Fundamentalism and American Culture*, pp. 52–55 for a description of this.

29. Ibid., p. 129.

30. Arno C. Gaebelein, quoted ibid., p. 143.

31. William L. Gaylord, The Soldier God's Minister, "A Discourse Delivered in the Congregational Church, Fitzwilliam, N.H., Sabbath Afternoon, October 5, 1862, on the Occasion of the Departure of a Company of Volunteers for the Seat of War," quoted in James H. Moorhead, *American Apocalypse: Yankee Protestants and the Civil War,* 1860–1869 (New Haven and London: Yale University Press, 1978), p. ix.

32. Ibid., p. x.

33. Ibid.

34. Tim LaHaye, *The Battle For the Mind*, p. 218.

35. Ibid. Emphasis added.

36. Jerry Falwell, *Listen, America!* p. 67 and throughout.

37. Ibid.

38. Ibid., p. 73.

39. Ibid., p. 114.

40. Ibid., p. 84.

41. Ibid., p. 97.

42. Ibid.

43. Hal Lindsey, *The Late Great Planet Earth*, p. 155.

44. Ibid., p. 158.

45. Ibid., pp. 159–160.

46. Ibid., p. 163.

47. Ibid., p. 163.

48. Ibid., p. 164.

49. Jerry Falwell, *Listen, America!* p. 98.

50. Ibid.

51. Ibid., p. 18.

52. Edward H. Flannery, *The Anguish of the Jews: Twenty-Three Centuries of Anti-Semitism* (New York: The Macmillan Co., 1965), p. xi.

53. F. Lovsky, *Antisémitisme et Mystère d'Israel* (Paris: Michel, 1955), p. 113.

54. Raul Hilberg, *The Destruction of the European Jews* (Chicago: Quadrangle

Books, 1961), pp. 3–4. Hilberg points out the parallels in Church rulings and Nazi laws and practices on pp. 5–6.

55. A. Roy Eckardt, *Elder and Younger Brothers* (New York: Schocken, 1973), p. 12.

56. Guibert of Nogent, quoted in Flannery, op. cit., pp. 90–91.

57. Ibid., p. 92.

58. Edward H. Flannery, *The Anguish of the Jews*, p. 93.

59. Martin Marty, *Righteous Empire*, pp. 24, 33.

60. Quoted ibid., p. 28.

61. Jerry Falwell, *Listen, America!* p. 63.

62. Quoted ibid., p. 13.

63. Ibid., p. 66.

64. Ibid.

65. Daniel Maguire, *A New American Justice: Ending the White Male Monopolies* (Garden City, New York: Doubleday, 1980), pp. 136–140.

66. Leonard Goodwin, *Do the Poor Want to Work?: A Social-Psychological Study of Work Orientation* (Washington, D.C.: The Brookings Institute, 1972), p. ix.

67. Tim LaHaye, *The Battle For the Mind*, pp. 9–10.

68. Ibid., p. 208. See also pp. 174, 197.

69. See Jerry Falwell, *Listen, America!* p. 225.

70. Richard Hofstadter, *The Paranoid Style in American Politics*, p. 21.

71. Martin Marty, *Righteous Empire*, p. 51.

72. J.M. O'Neill, *Religion and Education Under the Constitution*, p. 27.

73. Ibid. The quote on Kenrick is from Ray A. Billington, *The Protestant Crusade* (New York: The Macmillan Co., 1938), p. 221.

74. David Edwin Harrell, Jr., "The Roots of the Moral Majority," p. 5.

75. Richard John Neuhaus, "The Right to Fight," *Commonweal* 108, October 9, 1981, p. 557.

76. Quoted ibid.

77. Ibid.

78. "Baptist Shuns Catholic Schlafly," *Tampa Tribune*, January 29, 1980, p. 3a.

79. Jerry Falwell et al., *The Fundamentalist Phenomenon*, p. 47. Emphasis added.

80. Ibid., p. 145.

81. Ibid., pp. 146–47.

82. Tim LaHaye, *The Battle For the Mind*, p. 29.

Chapter Five

1. Allan J. Mayer et al., "A Tide of Born-Again Politics," p. 31.

2. 96th Congress, 1st Session, S. 1808, under amendments to the General Education Provisions Act 440B (3). Emphasis added.

3. Quoted in Ashley Montague, *The Natural Superiority of Women*, new rev. ed. (New York: Collier Books, 1974), pp. 28–29.

4. Paul Laxalt, *Congressional Record* 125, no. 127, September 27, 1979.

5. Ibid.

6. Ibid.

7. Tim LaHaye, *The Battle For the Mind,* p. 198.

8. Rosemary Ruether, "Politics and the Family," p. 262.

9. *Roe v. Wade,* 410 U.S. 113 (1973) and *Doe v. Bolton,* 410 U.S. 179 (1973).

10. Joseph Donceel, S.J., *Abortion in a Changing World* (New York and London: Columbia University Press, 1970), pp. 42–44.

11. Charles E. Curran, *Politics, Medicine and Christian Ethics* (Philadelphia: Fortress, 1973), p. 131.

12. "Abortion: Protestant Perspectives" *Encyclopedia of Bioethics* vol. I, ed. Warren T. Reich (New York and London: The Free Press, Collier, 1978), p. 15.

13. "Abortion: Contemporary Debate in Philosophical and Religious Ethics," ibid., p. 25.

14. "Abortion: Roman Catholic Perspectives," ibid., p. 9.

15. James J. Diamond, M.D., "Abortion, Animation and Biological Hominization," *Theological Studies* 36, June 1975, p. 312.

16. Ibid., p. 311, note 12.

17. Mary Anne Warren, Daniel Maguire, and Carol Levine, "Can the Fetus be an Organ Farm?" *Hastings Center Report* 8, October 1978, p. 23.

18. Ibid., p. 24.

19. Daniel C. Maguire, *Death by Choice* (Garden City, New York: Doubleday, 1974), pp. 186–87.

20. Frances Fitzgerald, "The Triumphs of the New Right," *The New York Review of Books,* November 19, 1981, p. 21.

21. See "The So-Called 'Human Life' Amendment," a short pamphlet published by American Civil Liberties Union Foundation, 132 W. 43rd St., New York, N.Y. 10036.

22. Senator Paul Laxalt, *Congressional Record,* vol. 125, no. 127, September 27, 1979.

23. See Daniel C. Maguire, *A New American Justice.*

24. Jerry Falwell, *Listen, America!* p. 108.

25. *The Family Protection Act,* Sec. 508.

26. Ibid., Sec. 506 (12).

27. Anthony Kosnik et al., *Human Sexuality: New Directions in American Catholic Thought* (New York, Paramus, Toronto: Paulist Press, 1977), p. 97.

28. John Boswell, *Christianity, Social Tolerance and Homosexuality* (Chicago and London: The University of Chicago Press, 1980), p. 269.

29. Kosnik et al., *Human Sexuality,* p. 198.

30. Jerry Falwell, *Listen, America!* pp. 158–60.

31. Kosnik et al., *Human Sexuality,* p. 187.

Conclusion

1. The Reverend Howard Hartzell, pastor emeritus of First Baptist Church in Philadelphia, has in his sermons preached powerfully against the embarrassing perversion of the Baptist tradition by the Falwellian Baptists.

2. Jerry Falwell et al., *The Fundamentalist Phenomenon,* p. 179.

3. Ibid., pp. 179–80.

4. Ibid., p. 180.

5. Ibid., pp. 180–81.

6. Ibid., pp. 181–82.

7. Ibid., p. 182.

8. Ibid., p. 183–84.

9. The address for Americans for Common Sense is 1825 Connecticut Avenue, Suite 216, Washington, D.C. 20009.

10. People for the American Way, 1015 18th Street N.W., Suite 310, Washington, D.C. 20030.

11. Moral Alternatives, 2419 E. Kenwood Blvd., Milwaukee, Wisconsin 53211.

INDEX